Mechell,

Thank you so
much for the
love & support!!

— Andy

PRAISE

An exciting call to action and a unique behind the scenes view of what it takes to thrive as an educator and leader in today's current K12 education system. Canlé reveals the myriad shifts to every day thinking that together inspire a renewed sense of hope starting with the belief that we are all an active part of the process of change. From visualization to authenticity, Canlé shows how slight shifts to your thinking open the door to larger shifts to your work each day in school.

Dr. Lindsay Portnoy
Cognitive Scientist & Associate Teaching Professor at Northeastern University
Author of Game On? Brain On! & Designed to Learn

I love this book! Andrew Canlé lays it out perfectly for educators in this easy, practical, and empowering read. He shares stories, research, and simple steps to power through the challenges that so many educators face. After reading Mindset Moments, I feel more energized and equipped to handle and overcome the barriers that hold us back. Andrew nailed it in this book!

Andrew Marotta
NY Principal | Author | Speaker
Leader of the #SurviveThrive Movement

Andrew Canlé has done a masterful job in creating Mindset Moments just in time! Mindset Moments provides easy access for students and adults to the theories, methods, and tools that everyone requires to navigate successfully through today's turbulent times! Brilliant!

Rich Hawkins, Ed.D.
Director of Educational Leadership, The College of St. Rose
Co-author of Designing School Systems for All Children

Mindset Moments is a powerful resource for educators that provides pathways to teach the core of growth mindset. The combination of the challenges embedded and video resources provide a call to action for both students and educators!

Jessica Ryan
Co-author of Growing a Growth Mindset: Unlocking Character Strengths Through Children's Literature

Mindset Moments outlines not just ideas, but true action steps that educators can take to overcome struggles and refocus as they pursue their passion and purpose. The framework and outline of this book allow for deep reflection of thought-provoking questions, solution-oriented ideas, and the opportunity to apply our learning and discoveries to our work. You will find yourself implementing these Mindset Moments strategies immediately in all areas of your life, both professional and personal.

Kelly Hoggard
Educator | Mentor
Author of Champ for Kids

Mindset Moments challenges educators to confront mental barriers and envision a clear and authentic pathway for success. Through his own personal and professional experiences, Andrew has created a framework that empowers educators to be our best selves and begin making a profound impact for generations to come.

Teresa Eberle
Elementary Educator

Mindset Moments is just what students and educators need to navigate today's challenges and be the best versions of themselves. In a world full of naysayers and rich with negativity, Mindset Moments provides a user-friendly framework for overcoming personal and professional challenges and achieving success while focusing on the positive and repelling the negative. Andrew masterfully drives home how the power of positive thinking can lead us all down the path to success together!

Jan Granger
Elementary Educator

Mindset Moments sets the path for us to become the best lead learners for our students and provides a concise road map to metacognitively achieve success. Andrew's framework will provide you with the spark needed to overcome challenges and achieve your best reality!

Melissa Gangi
Elementary Educator

In Mindset Moments, Andrew sends a clear and powerful message that we are only as limited as we allow ourselves to be. As educators, it is easy to get discouraged by all that we are asked to accomplish day in and day out. By the end of this book, you will have a renewed confidence to regain control of your mindset in a positive way and feel encouraged to keep going. I highly recommend this book as a must-read for anyone who desires to be their best self so that we can in turn inspire the same mindset in future generations.

Emily Paschall
Educator | Speaker
Author of Eyes on Culture: Multiply Excellence In Your School

From reinventing yourself to finding belief in the work you do, Mindset Moments will help you bring thoughts to action in your work with students, teachers, and parents. The stories are real and the challenges give you a practical pathway to improving your own mindset while empowering those around you.

Joe Sanfelippo
School Superintendent | Speaker
Co-author of Hacking Leadership

We often practice thinking patterns that reap the same outcome. Yet we wonder...why am I not getting the result I desire? In Mindset Moments, Andrew J. Canlé provides a systematic, sustainable framework to shape our thinking. These steps help shift one's reasoning from what seems impossible to focus more around what is within our realm of control. Throughout the pages, he presents personal stories to demonstrate ten Mindset Moments, using the framework, to model making this practice our own and empowering those we serve to do the same. Are you tired of thinking the same way and getting the same old result? Do your brain a favor, pick up Mindset Moments and create a lifelong shift in how you reflect and perform.

Tara M. Martin
Educator | Author | International Keynote Speaker
Director of Personal Relations and Communication , DBC Inc.

MINDSET MOMENTS

ANDREW J. CANLÉ

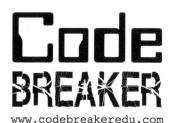

www.codebreakeredu.com

To life's obstacles.
You're great practice.

ACKNOWLEDGEMENTS

"Will you be in the rocking chair?"

When I was a kid I was afraid to sleep alone. My mother, the saint that she is, would sit in a rocking chair at the foot of my bed until I fell asleep without fail. Trust me, I'd diligently check every few minutes to see if she kept true to her word. She never let me down.

She always was, still is, and always will be there for me. For that, I am eternally grateful.

She and my father remain stalwart supporters of my sisters and I to this day but many haven't been so fortunate. My deck of cards landed me in a safe home surrounded by a community of mentors, coaches, doctors, and teachers you'll hear about as you work your way through these pages.

We cannot choose our parents, where we are born or what we are born into but we can choose our mindset. It's human for us to want to help others and the conversation we are about to have with one another is my way of outwardly extending positive energies to help you be at your best.

I'm the living and breathing hard work of many benefactors personified and the framework I share with you is their creation as much as it is my own. The words found within this guide serve to remind you that you're not alone and when times seem tough I encourage you to revisit this very sentence and remember that these words are here for you. I am here for you. Mindset Moments are here for you.

Like my mentors and caretakers throughout life, Brian Aspinall gave me the motivational zest to accept a new challenge and give this a shot. I'm flattered, humbled and excited to present to you my version of being in the rocking chair for you: Mindset Moments.

TABLE OF CONTENTS

FOREWORD

"Why don't I make a series of videos to help kids cultivate a positive mindset through weekly focus questions? They can serve as a jumping off point for teachers to spark class discussions."

Like many of Andrew's ideas, I told him it had potential, and it left my mind for the rest of the day.

Not his.

Luckily for the rest of the world, Andrew Canlé's mind doesn't work like ours. He operates differently. Most people would never take that next step of spending dozens of hours and a lot of sweat equity to create the videos that may have brought you to this book.

If you've never seen a Mindset Moment of the Week, they are short motivational clips that leave us saying, "Huh, I never thought of it like that!" Each video highlights a life lesson combined with a fun anecdote usually from Andrew's life or a recognizable figure that helps drive the week's message home. Before exiting stage right he provides the viewer with a prompt to focus on during the week and follows it up by delivering the fan favorite tagline: "Think about it...I'll see you later."

Many teachers have extended the initial concept way further than Andrew could have ever imagined, myself included. To this day he beams with joy whenever teachers tag him on social media using his content in a variety of ways. This is what earns a guy like Andrew Canlé the title of "Stellar Educator" in my book. He took a good idea and quickly turned it into something to help thousands of teachers and children. I can't tell you what makes him happier than helping people. He'd give you the shirt off his back.

I met Andrew 10 years ago through a group of mutual friends. He's 6 years older than me but sometimes it feels like 60 because of the diverse life experiences this man has packed into his years. He is one of those guys that I learn something new about every time we hang out. I used to bat an eye when he'd nonchalantly drop bombshells like "that was the time when I starred in Anton Chekhov's *The Seagull Off-Broadway*" or "I travelled there when my soccer team was ranked #1 in the United States." Now, it's just become a normal part of knowing Andrew.

With that being said, I do think his many life experiences are the catalyst for what has made him such a great teacher and what currently makes him a great administrator and motivator. If you examine some of these life experiences a bit deeper, you can see where his driven personality comes from.

Andrew grew up in a soccer family filled with celebrated careers. I remember hearing of his feats and passing Canlé plaques in our high school lobby. His dad was a respected player and coach and the family name was well known in the soccer scene. Imagine this and then discovering he battled a childhood medical condition that threatened his ability to walk earlier in his life.

After being diagnosed with Legg-Calve-Perthes disease (he'll explain this a lot better than I can in Mindset Moment #7), he spent his formative elementary years on crutches, sitting in the nurse's office while his friends played outside at recess. Keep in mind this wasn't for a few weeks or months, which feels like an eternity when you're that young. This was for multiple years. He received physical therapy every day FOR YEARS. His mother received training so she could give him his therapy seven days a week, three hundred sixty five days a year, FOR

YEARS. He went through loads of hardship and frustration both in and out of school during that time.

Why am I telling you this? Because facing adversity is the reason I think Andrew has become the success story that he is and why his voice resonates with so many. After hundreds of hours of therapy and hard work, Andrew was able to conquer his medical condition and play the sport he loved. He took the same drive and determination that he put into the recovery to become a decorated athlete.

I think this setback he experienced as a kid is the reason he has done so much in his life and has become, in my opinion, a beloved Renaissance man in the world of education. Besides athletic accomplishments and well-deserved educational awards, he's acted in commercials and movies (go search "ballroom dancing scene Step Up 3D" on YouTube and you'll find the author of this book dancing away), and he has released multiple albums as a singer/songwriter. He's put his own life on hold to fly across the United States for students and publicly posts his number and devotes time to anyone who reaches out. This is who he is. When Andrew Canlé says he's going to do something - he does it.

His energy is magnetic and I've never seen anyone not captivated by him or his teachings. He pays it forward 24/7 and enjoys every minute of helping others.

I'm not telling you these things to brag about my best friend— I'm telling you these things to stress that if anyone was going to encourage you or your kids to live life to the fullest and not let setbacks knock you down, Andrew Canlé is the perfect guy to do it.

Anthony Longo
Elementary School Teacher
Lifelong Friend

A 10-PART CREDO FOR EDUCATORS TO ACHIEVE THEIR BEST REALITY

Teaching can be the highest of highs and the lowest of lows. Our profession calls for the wearing of many hats ranging from the obvious roles of teacher, learner, mentor, coach, caretaker and friend, to the not so obvious roles of motivational speaker, comedian, detective, therapist, arbitrator, salesperson, interior designer, public figure, and the list goes on. These overt and covert roles generate specific challenges that take a toll on educators as evidenced by high levels of stress, burnout, and a deterioration of mental well-being affecting our mindset, pedagogy, and ultimately, student outcomes.

Mindset Moments are the solution.

Mindset Moments allow us to see things differently to enhance our condition and get better results! A Mindset Moment is an "Aha!" or jolt of eureka producing renewed outlook. It's a metacognitive practice helping us think about our thinking to transform our approach and guide us from point A to point B feeling rejuvenated and confident in our abilities to conquer adversity. Mindset Moments are the pathway leading us from our current reality to our desired future. They are about hope, dreams, and persistence. They are the tools we can use to combat the temptation of giving up and ultimately persevere. They are a framework from which to operate in order to achieve a vision of success.

When the odds seem stacked against us and negativity creeps in, sometimes all it takes is a shift in perspective to pull us out of the doldrums and revisit an obstacle through a new lens. This book serves as a strategy guide to do just that.

What if there was a way to recalibrate our thinking to endure any challenge?

What if despite the circumstance we could be at our best for ourselves, our colleagues, and kids?

We can through the use of this framework:

MINDSET MOMENT #1 - VISUALIZE
- Define what success looks like to you and consider the preparations needed in order to attain it.

MINDSET MOMENT #2 - CONTRIBUTE
- What energies are you exuding and how are they contributing something positive to help others and yourself be successful?

MINDSET MOMENT #3 - REPRESENT
- Who do you represent outside of yourself and how does your attitude impact them?

MINDSET MOMENT #4 - COMPETE
- Confront your mental barriers. To what extent have you reinforced areas of strength?

MINDSET MOMENT #5 - BE FEARLESS
- What is your motivation to keep going?

MINDSET MOMENT #6 - PERSEVERE
- Consider how close you are to success. What's holding you back?

MINDSET MOMENT #7 - REFRAME
- How can you turn criticism into motivation and problems into opportunities?

MINDSET MOMENT #8 - BE AUTHENTIC
- Are you being the best version of yourself or are you trying to be someone else?

MINDSET MOMENT #9 - POSITION
- How do you maintain a learner's approach?

MINDSET MOMENT #10 - FOLLOW THROUGH
- Repel negativity with the resilience to follow through.

Educators are a passionate and conscientious group who experience internal and external pressures on a daily basis. My hope is that upon completion of this book you feel more readily able to face any obstacle that the educational stratosphere presents and can be at your best to deliver a quality educational experience for all of your learners.

Are you ready to dive into this 10-part credo to achieve your best reality and transform both personal and professional relationships, achievement, and overall culture within your classroom, school, and beyond?

Let's get started!

VISUALIZE

As human beings it's no secret that we have hopes, aspirations, and dreams. As educators it's no secret that we have hopes, aspirations, and dreams for our students, too! We want nothing more than to see each child leave our classroom at the end of the school year better off than when they first entered. All too often, however, peripheral demands and challenges hinder our ability to devote ample individualized time to satisfy every learner's needs. On top of conventional job duties like delivering instruction to facilitate student learning, educators abound balance keeping pace with scope and sequences and targeting areas of student need, providing for overloaded classrooms with insufficient resources, and needing support from administrators who are faced with seemingly insurmountable barriers to pulling off a level of adequacy in the workplace in general. At some point, we eventually feel overwhelmed despite our best intentions to deliver a high quality educational experience. This sum total contributes to us academic professionals often losing our commander's intent, or focus on overall purpose and goals.

It's a familiar narrative and one that we know all too well. So, what's the solution?

How can K-12 professionals stay focused on desired outcomes amid the hodgepodge of difficulties that obstruct our ability to perform at a high level?

The solution resides within the following 3-step process detailed in this Mindset Moment: visualizing success by defining what it looks like, being honest with ourselves about the current circumstances, and preparing a plan to get from point A of our current reality to point B of our desired future.

STEP 1: VISION

DEFINING WHAT SUCCESS LOOKS LIKE AND FORMULATING THE VISION OF OUR DESIRED FUTURE

Our minds are powerful and when we visualize success it often happens. Visualization, in its simplest and most basic form, is a mental rehearsal technique used in much the same way that positive affirmations are for attaining a desired result. Where affirmations speak results into existence, visualizations picture them in our mind to be true prior to their materialization in the real world. Using visualization to depict a clear vision of what we aim to achieve is a worthwhile exercise when trying to keep our eye on the prize.

Visualization is a widely used technique in the sports world. In fact, many teams of various sports disciplines have engaged players in visualization practice as a means to reduce anxiety and build confidence and motivation prior to game time. Research supports the effectiveness of this practice. One popular study conducted by Dr. Judd Biasiotto at the University of Chicago made a convincing case for the merit of using visualization. The study lasted one month and consisted of three student groups with the first practicing basketball free throws, the second merely visualizing themselves making the free throws, and the third not practicing or thinking about shooting free throws at all. The third group showed no improvement but the results between the first and second group showcased the power of visualization. The first group improved by 24 percent while the second group improved 23 percent without ever even touching a basketball. In short, if "we believe it - we can achieve it" and I can personally attest to the value of this mantra.

I remember playing soccer for St. John's University back in 2006. The men's soccer program was ranked number 4 overall in the United States and we were contenders in the Big East Conference that year. Expectations were high and our team makeup was extremely atypical for any collegiate sport. I was one of fourteen freshmen that made up the roster of eighteen players; we were a very young and inexperienced squad; underdogs, if you will.

I vividly recall travelling to Akron, Ohio for a game against the Zips and a sports psychologist leading our team into an empty conference room devoid of tables and chairs. We were instructed to find a space on the floor to sit and close our eyes and the psychologist began the exercise prompting us to describe what was going to happen later that day in the game. It was the first visualization experience for many of us. Here is an example of the exchange:

Psychologist: What is your goal today?
Me: To win the game.
Psychologist: How do you intend to accomplish this?
Me: I intend to do my job.
Psychologist: And what is your job, exactly?
Me: To not let anyone beat me to the ball and to help my team score.
Psychologist: The ball is now at your feet. Do you see anyone to pass it to?
Me: Yes. I will pass it up the field and continue my run to support my teammate.
Psychologist: Good job. Did you get the ball back from your teammate?
Me: Yes, he passed the ball back to me because he saw me running down the sideline. I'm now crossing the ball into the middle so we can score a goal.

I can't tell you if we won or if I even saw any playing time that day but the point is that I felt supremely confident in making those visualizations come to fruition in the actual game. The exercise left us all feeling like it was entirely possible to attain what we had envisioned in that empty conference room. Our team discussion following the exercise revolved around how to make our visions come true no matter the obstacles. Our team continued to practice visualization throughout the season and won the Big East Conference Tournament that year.

Formulating a vision of your desired future outcome is the first step in visualizing and attaining success despite the odds or circumstances. Starting with the end in mind and working our way backwards is the key to achieving a new reality. The students in Dr. Biasotto's study would define success as making a free throw. My teammates and I would define success as winning the game against the Akron Zips. In order to achieve our goal, we must first define what it is and what it looks like.

What does this have to do with teaching?

It's safe to say that the overarching goal for any educator is overall student success. At least for the sake of this book and the journey for which you are about to embark, we'll assume this to be the case and therein lies a desired future outcome; 100% of students being successful regardless of any impediments to educators being able to perform job responsibilities.

What does this mean? What does, "100% of students being successful" look like? This is the crux of the first step in visualizing success: defining success.

Professionals in the academic arena engage in this type of work every single day with a salient example being lesson plans. A lesson objective or learning target such as, "I will be able to find the percent of a number" clearly defines success for both teachers and students; by the end students are expected to demonstrate their ability to find a percent of a number and teachers are to check for understanding along the way. The desired outcome acts as a guiding light ensuring the purpose of the instructional block remains intact and is ultimately accomplished.

Other lofty examples of this include:

By the end of the school year, every child in the class will have improved their reading proficiency level.

At the end of the first marking period, every child in the class will have adopted a growth mindset.

By June, every child will have included higher level vocabulary words in oral and written responses.

So on and so forth.

The point is that in order to beat the odds, overcome circumstances, defeat obstacles, and attain desired future outcomes, it's imperative the destination be clear and defining success is the initial step and catalyst for positive change.

Visualizing success means that a clear picture of the end goal has been fully formulated in our mind's eye. In the case of the aforementioned lesson example of finding the percent of a number, recognizing our starting point prior to any first attempts at mastery is key. In other words, what are students bringing into the lesson in terms of prior knowledge? How far is it from their starting point to the desired future outcome of finding the percent of a number? And, how do we get them there? A spiral review to check for prerequisite skill of benchmark fractions or ratios to inform our approach and scaffold learning may be something to consider, in this instance. In order for this to occur, however, we must first be honest about our collective starting point.

STEP 2: HONESTY

BEING TRANSPARENT WITH OURSELVES WHEN ASSESSING THE CURRENT REALITY

Let's consider the following analogy to break down the necessary second tenet to achieve a desired future when visualizing success: honesty.

We all remember taking medicine as a kid and we despised the process. As a matter of fact, hardly anyone knows of someone who actually liked measuring out the exact dosage of cough syrup in that funny plastic cup and having to brace for impact while every part of the medicinal compound was tasted on the way down. Yeah, that process. We know it very well and had a passionate disdain for it as children, with some of us carrying that into adulthood, myself included.

Think of being honest with yourself in much the same way as taking medicine as a kid; hardly anyone likes doing it because it's difficult to swallow down but in the end we're usually better off. Being truthful with ourselves is the best medicine for growth because accurately assessing our current reality is a critical step toward achieving our hopes and dreams.

What does this look like?

Assessing our current reality is an exercise in using vulnerability as the catalyst for change. For educators, this often means knowing our students, understanding the environment within which we're operating, and truly knowing ourselves. That is to say, asking ourselves the following questions: What are my students' skill levels and abilities? What are the resources readily available to me that I can use to help my learners grow? What are my current capabilities as a lead learner and how can I improve to usher student growth?

Conducting an audit of the current situation is in our best interest in order to understand our starting point. This informs us of how far away or close to the desired future we are and once our start and end points are identified, the planning and preparation to enhance our condition and mitigate any hindrances or obstructions along the pathway to achieving our vision of success begins!

STEP 3: PLANNING

CONSIDERING THE PLANNING AND PREPARATION NEEDED TO GO FROM OUR CURRENT REALITY TO OUR DESIRED FUTURE

The third step of the process ties it all together.

Let's consider the rudimentary example of children being asked, "What do you want to be when you grow up?" It's a question we've been asked at some point during our early years and it's safe to say that many of us had clear answers ranging from the practical to the not so practical. Common answers might've included doctors, teachers, or professional sports stars. Other responses may have been velociraptors, queens reigning over kingdoms, or ninjas. While some of us may have succeeded in our pursuits, many of us have not. The question becomes, why?

The answer is fairly obvious: lack of planning.

Commit the 6 P's to memory: Proper Prior Planning Prevents Poor Performance.

We rarely were asked any questions surrounding, "What do you want to be when you grow up?" We provided our answer and the conversation usually ended. We didn't consider a follow-up question such as, "How do you plan on achieving this?" or the lead in question of, "What are you in the present moment?" which would've shed light on how far we had to go to achieve our goal. Perhaps by asking ourselves, "Who am I now? Who do I want to become? And, how do I achieve that?" we could've been more successful in our original pursuits. Although it is highly unlikely you'd become a velociraptor, but I digress.

The formula is quite simple:

Attaining Success (as defined by us) = Identifying our starting point + Understanding the steps needed to actualize our vision

The University of Chicago students knew their end goal of making free throws and used visualization to improve their skill-set by 23 percent. The St. John's University men's soccer team had a vision of what success was and practiced daily to become Big East Champions. Students trying to find a percent of a number could use prerequisite skills to achieve the learning target. In each case, success is clearly defined, starting points are understood, and a plan is put in place to travel from the starting point to achieving the vision of success.

Mindset Moment #1 focuses on the macro and broad scale of visualizing success overall. As we progress, we will dive deeper into Mindset Moments that address the micro and more granular perspectives to recalibrate our thinking and be at our best.

MINDSET MOMENT CHALLENGE #1

DEFINE WHAT SUCCESS LOOKS LIKE TO YOU AND
CONSIDER THE PREPARATIONS NEEDED IN
ORDER TO ATTAIN IT.

REC

00:00:01   BE PREPARED [S1 E9]

REC

00:00:01   VISUALIZE SUCCESS [S2 E1]

CONTRIBUTE

MINDSET MOMENT #2

CONTRIBUTE

Educators, by definition, act as de facto caretakers of children as well as one another. It's in our DNA to innately want to be there for others and provide a shoulder to lean on during trying times. It's perhaps this nurturing perspective that led many of us to become educators in the first place; to support those in need. However, a comforting shoulder to cry on may not be enough when students and colleagues are struggling to succeed in their endeavors. In fact, it's usually too late since it's applied retroactively to a given situation. In order to truly help others we must consider how we can contribute a lasting positive impact beforehand to lessen any struggles along the road of actualizing a vision of success.

Mindset Moment #1 spoke of defining success in order to achieve desired outcomes. Here, we focus on contributing to the actualization of a shared vision as it relates to a class of students, team of educators, or any type of group working together to achieve a goal in general.

Mindset Moment #2 focuses on the process of "How".

Specifically, how can we contribute something positive to help others and ourselves be successful? This question generates a framework predicated on the following three pillars: thinking proactively, demonstrating value to help actualize a collective vision of success and practicing empathy to enhance teamwork.

STEP 1: THINK PROACTIVELY

ACTIVELY COMMUNICATING AND PLANNING THROUGH FORESIGHT

Being proactive, for all intents and purposes, is a skill that is developed over time and usually comes with situational experience. Whether an inexperienced newbie or a seasoned veteran, considering the intended and unintended consequences of our actions and inactions is the secret sauce for making valuable contributions in connection with achieving the desired outcomes of the group at large. In other words, anticipation and prediction are our friends.

Let's consider the following two versions of the same scenario:

Version 1: A 5th grade physical education class opens with the teacher telling students to grab a jump rope. While explaining that jumping rope is an aerobic exercise connected to the class's overall study of coordination and fitness, a student begins jumping rope and accidentally strikes a nearby peer.

Version 2: A 5th grade physical education class opens with the teacher telling students to find an open space and wait to receive a jump rope. Before handing out the jump ropes, the teacher models proper form and spacing and the lesson rolls on without a hitch.

Enter the power of prevision.

Thinking proactively is about prevision, or anticipating what is to come. This is not to say that we're to worry about and react to everything given the fact that many things fall outside our locus of control. Rather, thinking proactively is about focusing our time and energies on what we can control, like communication and planning.

We can agree that Version 2 is the exemplar, the difference being the absence of foresight exercised in Version 1. A third version altogether is the teacher flipping their lid and panicking with regard to unruly students getting injured on their watch; this wouldn't be helpful either. The teacher in Version 2 proactively anticipated what may go wrong; a critical component of lesson planning and the facilitation of explicit instructions.

Lesson planning is a suitable example of a proactive measure educators take on a daily basis. By design, a well-thought-out lesson plan anticipates possible student misconceptions and accounts for scaffolding of learning to achieve an end result i.e., the learning target. Ideally, this is evidenced by 100% of students demonstrating skill acquisition, as mentioned in Mindset Moment #1.

Actively communicating and planning through foresight can generate the self-initiated behaviors needed to act in advance as opposed to reacting after an event has already transpired. Thinking about solutions to problems that may occur leads to profound previsions that can save everyone a lot of headaches and keep the collective vision of success a realistic outcome.

Asking ourselves the following question can help us maintain a proactive headspace:

How can I contribute something of positive value to help others and myself achieve the vision of success?

Let's define what we mean by, "contribute something positive" so we're all on the same page. This is not to be confused with toxic positivity, meaning that we merely act cheerful and ooze platitudes such as, "Don't worry, be happy!" and "Turn that frown upside down!" Instead, "contributing something positive" as it pertains to Mindset Moments means we demonstrate value that helps ourselves and the team be successful overall, by inching closer and closer to the desired future result. In essence, "Contribute something positive" is the answer to, "What do you bring to the table and how is it helping us come closer to success?"

STEP 2: DEMONSTRATE VALUE

ASSISTING IN THE ACTUALIZATION OF DESIRED OUTCOMES THROUGH POSITIVE CONTRIBUTIONS

"Are you physically and mentally prepared?"

I can still hear the low and calm treble of my Coach's voice, smell the synthetic turf field, feel the butterflies darting around my stomach, hear the rumble of the crowd, see the opportunity of the moment, and nearly taste the sweetness of victory as our pregame warmup ended and we headed to the locker room as one half of an amateur soccer match.

"When you all step on that field make sure you're contributing something positive to help the team win. Otherwise, what are you doing there?"

I was a teenager at that moment and the words my coach preached have stayed with me all these years later.

"Contribute something positive" is a concise sentiment that enabled us to self-evaluate and determine what we could do to help the team be successful. Personally, my speed was an asset whereas my teammates had size, strength, skill, etc. Adding all of these parts together to create a greater whole embodied the example of, "contributing something positive" to help us come out on top with a victory.

Just as each question during a lesson should help guide students to achieve the objective and acquire new skills, the metaphorical moves we make (or literal in the case of a soccer game) and what we bring to the table should bring the team (or students, grade level colleagues, school building, or school district) closer to achieving the vision of success.

Demonstrating our value also augments mutual trust. As educators, we are trusted lead learners tasked with guiding our students on a journey of discovering new skills through engaging awakenings of the mind and interesting challenges that test the mettle of one's grit, perseverance, and determination to achieve! This can be a tall order when working in isolation and having grade level teammates to rely on is a huge boost in self-efficacy, or our own belief in our ability to succeed.

Demonstrating one's value is the perfect confluence of individual and communal pursuits. The convergence of individual and team-oriented efforts bringing us closer to success and eventually attaining it to reach even greater heights is always the end goal.

But Andrew, what if I don't know how to demonstrate my value? I'm so glad you asked!

Remember that quality is subjective and one's trash is another's treasure, as the old adage goes. Put another way, we all have something positive to contribute and discovering the best in one another starts with empathy.

STEP 3: PRACTICE EMPATHY

ENHANCING TEAMWORK THROUGH MUTUAL UNDERSTANDING AND RESPECT

The Swedish retailer IKEA once launched an anti-bullying campaign centered on the effects of positive and negative talk. The brand's marketing team set up two plants in a school and told students to compliment one with praise and berate the other with insults.

We know where this is going: The praised plant thrived while the insulted plant wilted and withered.

The aim of the campaign was to demonstrate the destruction that negativity can cause. While the scientific community scoffs at the experiment's validity, the clever premise put forth by IKEA's marketing team retains its poignancy: be kind.

The controversial marketing stunt brought the importance of kindness to light and served to remind us of its long-lasting benefits. Moreover, thinking of others is a form of empathy and forging connections by spreading joy is one way we can contribute something positive.

I learned the value of being kind to others very early on in my life, second grade to be exact. I was in Mrs. Larsen's class at William L. Buck school in Valley Stream, New York, the first suburb outside the city boroughs on Long Island. It's a diverse, middle-class town filled with hard working and earnest people. We do not come from money nor wealth but find affluence in our pride to work hard and care for one another. It was around the holidays and I had the good fortune of being selected to pick from the illustrious prize box! There at the bottom of the magical suitcase lay the toy army soldiers I had saved up all my hard-earned reward points for over the first few months of the school year. You can imagine my eyes widening and hands trembling with excitement as I made my move to claim what was rightfully mine, shoving aside bouncy balls and other prizes I didn't show the light of day. Then, suddenly, peeking out from under the wooden paddle board I saw a cat shaped oven mitt. What I felt in that moment as a seven year old could only be expressed with a loving sigh and one word; empathy. I knew what I had to do. In an instant all of my hard work to amass enough points for the army toy soldiers washed away and every fiber of my being acknowledged it was the perfect gift for the love of my life; my mom.

I remember the interaction going something like this:

Mrs. Larsen: You have another minute left to choose a prize.
Me: How much for the glove?
Mrs. Larsen: You have enough, Andrew.
Me: I'll take it.

I was intuitive enough to decipher the scrunch of Mrs. Larsen's nose and furrow of her brow as utter confusion. Why would a sports-obsessed kid select a cat shaped oven mitt? It was only after I explained my reasoning that caused my second grade lead learner to melt before my eyes, a reaction I wouldn't understand until much later. After all, it was just an oven mitt for my mom. Not a big deal.

I couldn't have been more wrong as the oven mitt is a gift my mom still has, still loves, and still uses to this day. A simple gesture of kindness proliferated into lifelong positive impact.

This is the power of practicing empathy.

I knew the gift would be a hit but couldn't possibly foresee the degree of impact the simple gesture would have on my mom. The positive contribution made to her was long-lasting in many ways. Namely, it helped bring us closer together as mother and son and solidified our bond as a family unit.

Aside from the experience teaching me the value of spreading joy (albeit my understanding of it at the time was to shower girls with gifts and live like a Casanova), it taught me something else; practicing empathy is a choice well within our locus of control. Some sources even estimate the average adult to make around 35,000 choices a day. Imagine if a few of those choices were set aside and devoted towards uplifting our students and colleagues what we could accomplish together!

What can we do to help those around us grow and thrive?

It's a worthwhile question to consider when beginning our day because it holds us accountable for contributing something positive and progressing us toward achieving the vision of success.

Personal anecdotes aside, a famous example of instilling empathic values is Jane Elliott's Blue Eyes/Brown Eyes exercise with her third grade class in Iowa. In short, Elliott made the concept of prejudice concrete for her students through an experiment by making the brown-eyed children in the class feel superior and flipping the script for the blue-eyed children a few days later. What's perhaps most interesting is when the students felt superior they were able to complete their work more accurately and in half the time than when they were feeling inferior. This tells us that how others treat us affects us deeply and feeling good about ourselves really does matter.

The exercise was intended to shed light on and cultivate a deeper understanding of prejudice and is also a great example of the benefits of being kind and spreading joy. After all, thinking of others is a form of empathy and arguably the most powerful way to contribute positively to the greater good in order to attain desired future outcomes.

Why is this important for education professionals and schools?

Children feed off our energies and if we're not contributing something positive to help others thrive and achieve end goals, then our energies are steering away from productivity in the workplace and ultimately hampering student growth. Simply put, if we're not collegial with one another it's likely to have a negative impact on student learning either indirectly or directly. It's also likely that progress toward actualizing the vision of success will be more difficult to attain.

Being successful when you're shrouded in negativity or feeling isolated and alone is a rare feat. There are exceptions to the rule but the likely path of least resistance to accomplishment is making positive contributions that incrementally move us closer to our desired outcomes.

MINDSET MOMENT CHALLENGE #2!

WHAT ENERGIES ARE YOU EXUDING AND HOW ARE THEY CONTRIBUTING SOMETHING POSITIVE TO HELP OTHERS AND YOURSELF BE SUCCESSFUL?

REC

CONTRIBUTE SOMETHING POSITIVE [S1 E1]

SPREAD JOY [S1 E2]

BE KIND [S1 E7]

00:00:01 BE EXCELLENT TO EACH OTHER [S1 E16]

REPRESENT

MINDSET
MOMENT
#3

REPRESENT

Synonymous terms for educator might include public official or servant, although individuals not particularly fond of our ilk could probably think of something more colorful. As public officials serving our respective communities we represent more than ourselves, and our conduct inside and outside of the workplace matters. We're living reflections of our school values and our students are living reflections of our teaching. The daily energies we bring to our communities are micro-investments in the human capital all around us, and it's critically important that we build on previous successes. Still though, educators find themselves faced with disengaged students, cynical coworkers, and supervisors caught in a bureaucracy prioritizing the checking of superficial boxes deemed as best practices.

What's an educator to do? How can we stay on our A game and help others do the same?

Mindset Moment #3 proposes a solution using a simple framework referred to as the 3 I's: Ideas, Impact, and Inspiration.

The previous Mindset Moment illuminated how what we say and do can have a long-lasting impact on those around us. Mindset Moment #3 explains how to be the best versions of ourselves by linking our actions to ideas, aligning them to impact, and demonstrating how they can inspire others. This Mindset Moment delves into how we can best represent ourselves and the principles for which we stand.

STEP 1: IDEAS

ANCHOR ACTIONS TO AN IDEA

Tethering our actions to an idea can exploit a gap in how we think and shed new light on how to be our best selves.

By now you've noticed soccer was a huge part of my life growing up and molded me in many ways entering adulthood. I find the world of sports also makes for smooth analogies for our work as educators, so here's another:

Let's go back to my Coach's pregame message from Mindset Moment #2. We hit the field roaring and ready to go, each one of us trying our best to contribute to the team's overall success. We were completely outplayed and overmatched the entire first half of the game. Don't worry, his halftime speech was not as disappointing as our first-half performance, hence the fact that I've remembered it all these years later. Or, it's possible the memory remains alive and kicking (pun intended) due to the fact that my coach for the game was none other than Mike Windischmann. Doesn't sound familiar?

We've heard of the fictitious superhero, Captain America, yes? Mike Windischmann was literally captain America for the United States men's soccer team. In order to understand the magnitude of what this meant to us young players from the city streets of Queens, New York, allow me to explain some United States soccer history:

Mike Windischmann captained the men's team that ended the United States' forty year drought of qualifying for the World Cup, an international soccer tournament showcasing the highest levels of talent that captivates onlookers every four years. His name and soccer accomplishments are in the United States Soccer Hall of Fame, and what's more, he's from Queens, New York, which to a bunch of teenage boys from the area who loved soccer, made him a living legend, God incarnate, and cut from our same cloth to boot! Put another way, his words resonated with us.

I remember the halftime speech vividly as I crouched on the sideline winded. I even recall his outfit that day; Nike products head to toe (we were sponsored by Nike, my memory isn't that extraordinary). I remember hanging on his every word:

"Let me make this very clear so you all understand: When you step on that field, you're not just playing for yourself. You're playing for each other. You're playing for your friends and family. You're playing for your hometown. You're playing for your state and your country. When you step on that field you're more than just a jersey number. You represent much more than just yourself."

I immediately looked across the stadium and my eyes located my parents and sisters in attendance that day. I wanted to make them proud and win the game. I wanted to represent them the best I could.

This is what anchoring actions to an idea can accomplish. The halftime speech unearthed a gap in our mentality and elicited an emotional response that left us yearning to perform at our best. Captain America's words pierced through us and drove the idea of us representing more than ourselves home. Coach Windischmann anchored our actions to the idea that we represent others besides ourselves and must act accordingly. In the context of the game, we became tied to the desire to make our families proud of us.

When anchoring actions to an idea, some questions to consider might include the following:

What drives you and what impact do you want to have on others?

What guiding principle(s) do you consider to be an anchor?

What do you find yourself consistently remaining tethered to?

Believing we stand for something outside ourselves is a key component to individual and team success. Exposing our students to this type of thinking is especially powerful. Although we may not be World Cup participants or captains of our respective countries, our words as educators resonate far beyond the walls of our classrooms and school buildings. Our words stay with our students just as the words of our coaches and mentors have stayed with us over time. What's more, we create a powerful presence by anchoring to a belief coveted by the collective. It seldom matters what our particular status is when our "Why" aligns with the beliefs and values of others. When a student understands how a specific lesson will help them accomplish a personal goal or how it will enhance their tomorrow, we are on the right track for making a positive impact.

STEP 2: IMPACT

ALIGN ACTIONS TO IMPACT

Connecting our actions to the impact they have on us and others further affirms our path leads to positive lasting change.

A rhetorical question to you, the reader: do you have a set of classroom rules?

Perhaps we're all familiar with the traditional format:

No running
No calling out
Don't do this

Don't do that
No...
No...
No...
Don't...
Don't...
Don't...

Let's not mince words or beat around the bush: Rules stifle - Beliefs empower. Not many people enjoy being told what to do, but many people do enjoy being a part of something.

This is where impact comes to life.

Coach Windischmann's words not only tethered our actions to an idea but also made an impact on us.

What made the halftime speech so impactful?

Rereading his words you'll notice one very glaringly obvious difference between his phrasing and the syntax of the class rules above: He allowed us to come to our own realizations and helped us anchor our actions to an idea through discovery. He shed light on a new way of thinking with us not at the center of our universe. He addressed a collective mental gap and filled it with a new outlook and approach. We were pleased to oblige and felt empowered to take our fate into our own hands and be our best to represent others well by winning the game. Conversely, the class rules are a non-example and while they may still align actions to impact, they are mere authoritative dictation. They are a conversation killer, not a conversation starter. They leave no room for discovery and generate little impact as evidenced by students throughout the history of academia continuing to break the rules and teachers continuing to engage in power struggles.

I shifted my approach to classroom management during my 2nd year of teaching 6th graders at a 5-8 middle school in

East New York, Brooklyn. Building relationships and connecting with students came naturally to the point that they worked extremely hard for me. I took great pride in curating a productive learning space described by a former supervisor as a place of, "academic seriousness and collegiality." I fancied myself an effective teacher with respect to helping students achieve but knew deep down it was for my benefit and I hadn't tapped into the intrinsic levels for which I sought to reach. This was manifested in student behavioral problems outside of my class such as quarreling at lunch tables or in physical education class, art, music, etc. Put bluntly, if my presence wasn't felt, the values I instilled in my classroom vanished into thin air.

Educators share this pain and it stems from a lack of aligning actions to impact.

The point I'm making is that labeling my classroom rules as, "Classroom Guidelines for Success" made no difference in the grand scheme of things because it was a thin guise covering traditional rules rooted in dictation and compliance, not belief and empowerment. My students wanted to make me proud but did not consider making themselves proud. My classroom rules had finite impact and ended at the door leading into the hallway, them failing to understand they represented more than just themselves but caretakers, teachers, grade level, school, town, and beyond.

Where there is student failure, there is mentor failure, and so I looked inward.

For the rest of my teaching career I employed a different strategy referred to as classroom beliefs. There were two: "We always try our best and we always allow others to try their best." That was it.

How is this different from, "Classroom Guidelines for Success"?

The difference is subtle yet significant. The classroom beliefs aligned all actions to the impact they carried. Where rules make us compliant prisoners, beliefs liberate and empower us to help the team be successful. Beliefs allow us to represent a cause rather than being a compliant servant to an authoritative figure. It transitions our mentality from "them and us" to "we".

Let's look at an exchange that has occurred with a slouching student tapping their pencil loudly and distracting others:

Me: Anthony, are you trying your best?
Anthony: Yes, I'm just really tired.
Me: Sit up straight, it'll help open up your lungs and feed oxygen to your brain to wake you up!
Anthony: Ok.
Me: Are you allowing others to try their best? Meaning that you're not causing any distraction?
Anthony: Whoops, I didn't realize my pencil tapping was so loud.

The classroom beliefs tied all actions to their impact making them applicable to innumerable contexts and scenarios. In a short exchange Anthony made his own discoveries without any authoritative dictation coming from me, his teacher. He was able to realize he was a part of something bigger than himself; an entire class of learners trying to acquire new skills.

This strategy compounded over time and shifted control from me to my learners. The change was dramatic as my students year after year took onus of personal and collective responsibility, representing themselves and others to the best of their ability. Behavioral issues seemed to dissipate inside and outside of my classroom as students began connecting their actions to the potential positive or negative impact they could have on others such as their caretakers, classmates, or myself. They no longer operated from a heliocentric model with themselves at the center, but took on a broadened perspective concerning others. In short, it was a transformational shift and it was all because actions became aligned to their impact.

As stated earlier, not many people enjoy being told what to do, but many people do enjoy being a part of something and when beliefs are shared and we feel empowered that our actions have impact, the sky's the limit for making new realities come alive.

STEP 3: INSPIRATION

INSPIRE OTHERS THROUGH ACTION

Inspiring others through action embeds accountability with respect to representing the self and others as intended.

"Act as if someone's always watching."

Moving beyond any underlying creepiness this quote evokes lies a strong message: we inspire others when we lead by example. "Do as I say and not as I do" is not an advisable philosophy, especially when it comes to Mindset Moment #3. Our actions matter for the 3 I's to have any lasting positive effect.

Had I not embodied the classroom beliefs, it wouldn't have worked well. My students held one another accountable for upholding the classroom beliefs and acting accordingly to be a representation of such beliefs inside and outside of the classroom because I consistently led by example through action.

Had Mike Windischmann not been an example of what he preached at halftime it wouldn't have resonated as strongly. We wouldn't have shifted our thinking and approached the second half of the game with a renewed and inspired outlook aiming to honor all those we represented.

Putting our intentions into action is a prerequisite for the 3 I's to be effective and ultimately inspire others to make change.

During the large majority of the movie *The Truman Show*, Jim Carrey's character wasn't aware his every move was being watched. He didn't have the luxury that we do as educators being fully cognizant that we're in the public eye and molding young minds.

Students emulate our every move. They dress up as us on Halloween, they do hilarious impressions of us and they repeat our one liners at the dinner table. I recall walking down the hallway one day with my pen in my right ear, as is my usual style. A student approaching must've noticed and placed his pen in his right ear and kept walking. The smallest things we do can have major implications on young minds.

Use the 3 I's of ideas, impact, and inspiration to steer clear of cynicism and remain at the ready to be the best versions of ourselves and to inspire others to do the same.

In order for this to occur, however, we must first uncover our own areas of strength and weakness.

MINDSET MOMENT CHALLENGE #3!

WHO DO YOU REPRESENT OUTSIDE OF YOURSELF
AND HOW DOES YOUR ATTITUDE IMPACT THEM?

REC

00:00:01

AWESOME ATTITUDE [S2 E4]

COMPETE

Over the course of our careers we're asked to improve our skill-sets in any way, shape, or form to garner better results as measured by student achievement. Yet, capricious trends of the marketplace and boxed professional developments often miss the mark with respect to personalization of need and relevance to specific educator circumstances. Still, we do our best to implement triangular pegs into square holes with varying annual results until the next wave of "best practices" surface in the educational stratosphere. This flavor of the week, month, and year cycle fails to refine our abilities to mold young minds and our educational acumen hardly ever becomes enhanced unless we take the bull by the horns and seek out our own learning opportunities to better our practice.

The question becomes: How can educators continually augment their personal and professional growth in order to best service their community of learners?

It boils down to competition.

There's an interesting dichotomy in education between collaboration and competition. Coming together as professional learning communities to uplift one another is often juxtaposed against comparisons of individual triumphs and successes.

Therein lies the conundrum facing educators: How do we reconcile the stark difference between being team players and striving for personal growth?

The answer to satisfy both ends of the spectrum is to engage in the only meaningful and worthwhile competition there is: the competition within ourselves. When we improve ourselves the benefits are indirectly felt by others and can reverberate throughout the team.

Mindset Moment #4 takes a closer look at how to compete with ourselves by presenting the 3 strategy components of confronting mental barriers, reinforcing areas of strength, and avoiding comparisons.

Our world is ever-changing and our educational institutions reflect such societal transience. In order to sculpt young minds and turn dreams into realities, it's imperative that we're up to speed and grow our practice by competing with ourselves to be better each day.

STEP 1: CONFRONT MENTAL BARRIERS

COMMITTING TO ACTION

Before we can improve ourselves and help others we must first acknowledge how to be at our best. Confronting mental barriers is about understanding that we can go beyond what we believe to be our limitations. After all, we never know how much we can do until we just do it. There are countless examples spanning human history of going beyond our limits and reaching new heights but one milestone achievement comes to mind that strongly correlates to confronting mental barriers; Sir Roger Bannister breaking the 4-minute mile.

Mental barriers can hold us back and the 4-minute mile is an easily digestible example to reference. For decades the best and brightest sports minds considered the prospect of athletes running a mile in under 4 minutes to be all but impossible. At best, the track and field community thought there was only a sliver of hope in ideal running conditions for the most physically gifted and well trained athletes to reach the impenetrable and unbreakable feat of sub 4-minute status.

Alas, it was the most unlikely of runners, a full time student with no professional coaching to slay the unconquerable physical and mental barrier that plagued runners across the globe for years. On a cold and wet morning, Sir Roger Bannister ran a 3:59.4 mile, becoming the first person to ever run a mile in less than 4 minutes, shattering widely accepted conventions of what was thought to be possible for human beings.

Here's the kicker: Although the unbeatable 4-minute mile time stood undefeated for decades, once Bannister conquered the task many others followed suit. Since the record was broken there have been more than 1,000 other runners that have bested 4 minutes on the track.

Case in point: the floodgates open once mental barriers are broken and we can achieve much more than we initially think we can.

The Navy Seals refer to this notion of surpassing one's preconceived limitations as the 40 percent rule, meaning that when we think we've reached our point of exhaustion we've actually only tapped into about 40 percent of what we're capable of doing. Put in layman's terms, just because we haven't done it before doesn't mean we can't do it. Confronting mental barriers is as much a conduit for proving what is possible as it is a pathway to personal and professional growth.

This frame of mind pervades many different areas of life, too. It's not so uncommon that once a precedence is set by a given innovator, many others begin setting personal records as well. When we know it's possible, our mental barriers dissipate quite quickly.

We observe this change within students every year. Each new topic or skill presents what are perceived to be insurmountable challenges that overwhelm the young minds we service. They struggle to see how in the world they'll get over the hump and survive, yet they do time and again with our guidance.

I think back to my younger days of having my mind blown by multiplication, then algebra, then calculus, then finance, and on and on. Similarly, growing up, writing seemed like a chore in and of itself. From spelling tests, to paragraph writing, to essays, to multi-page papers and reports, have mercy on my soul! Each step presented challenges but it wasn't until I confronted my mental barriers that I was able to buckle down and conquer the material one step at a time.

Perhaps my early days of beating bosses at the final stage of video game levels ingrained this mindset into me but we truly never know how much we can do until we just do it. From there, new goals present themselves and we've grown our skill-sets and achieved new levels of mental toughness in no time!

Confronting our mental barriers is a competition within ourselves. Our intrapersonal conversations can be difficult but referencing Mindset Moment #1, honesty is the key. It's tough telling ourselves we can do more when we feel we've maxed out but sometimes that's the exact boost we need to convince ourselves of our own potential. Remember, we don't enjoy taking medicine but it makes us better off in the end. Be honest with yourself and don't run from mental barriers; confront and conquer them.

What's interesting to note is that Bannister almost didn't run the day he broke the 4-minute mile record. After a bout with indecisiveness, he confronted his mental barrier and set a record, further proving that personal growth is a mental chess match within ourselves with commitment playing a key role paving the way for change.

Competition can make most of us nervous and competing with ourselves to reach our full potential is no easy task. A bit of wisdom imparted to me by one of my coaches that I turn to when nerves bubble up is the following:

"Don't think about what it's for, just think about what has to get done."

Confronting mental barriers is about execution, doing rather than thinking or talking, competing with ourselves and removing tangential pressures from the equation to focus on the bottomline result.

Faced with a last second shot to win the game in the championship?

"Don't think about what it's for, just think about what has to get done." Focus on form, breathe, and trust your muscle memory and training to score.

Big assignment with major implications for your overall academic success?

"Don't think about what it's for, just think about what has to get done." Rely on your research and prove you know the content.

Interview for your dream job?

"Don't think about what it's for, just think about what has to get done." Dress to impress and be clear on why the team needs someone like you over all others.

Generational talent and artistic great, Pablo Picasso is attributed with saying, "action is the foundational key to all success." Confronting mental barriers hinges on the action of taking the first step toward personal and professional growth. Mustering up the courage to take action requires us to decipher which actions are points of leverage pertinent to transformational change.

STEP 2: REINFORCE STRENGTHS

MAKING OUR BRIGHT SPOTS BRIGHTER

"Play to your strengths" is a popular idiom that means we prioritize and give attention to the things that we do well, usually resulting in some form of success.

Playing to our strengths masks areas in need of improvement. The funny thing about magnifying strengths is that perceived weaknesses no longer matter as much. Baseball pitchers with unhittable fastballs don't need to worry about their lackluster curveball. Top selling bakers don't need to focus on their inability to cook risotto. Amazing inventors don't need to spend time transforming themselves into salespeople.

Expanding our repertoire of skills is a fantastic undertaking and this portion of Mindset Moment #4 is not trying to detract from such an aspiration whatsoever. Rather, the point is geared towards answering the following question:

In what areas do you feel most competent and to what extent can you strengthen those levels of self-efficacy?

Focusing on areas in need of improvement takes away from opportunities to build upon already existing competencies we possess. Simply put, make your bright spots brighter. For educators, playing to our strengths is our greatest asset.

How do I find out what my strengths are if I'm unsure?

One way is film study.

There's a reason the billion dollar world of sports invests time, money, and lots of energy into watching playback of games; it works (I understand this can be polarizing so feel free to substitute film study with feedback if you have a willing party to help out and observe your practice).

Watching ourselves on film is a transformative experience that teaches us a lot about ourselves and highlights areas of strength. Moving beyond the initial jarring feelings of vulnerability, it allows us to assemble major takeaways to improve our classroom practice.

When I videotaped myself, I came away with amazing bits of information I wouldn't have been aware of had I not hit the record button. Here is a takeaway that transformed my personal practice early on:

According to evaluators, my use of prescriptive questioning throughout lessons helped guide learners towards achieving the learning target. However, I struggled at times to reach 100% of students and so I turned to the video playback with the following question in mind:

How could I reach 100% of students more consistently in my classroom?

The first thing I realized soon after video analysis was that I had a tendency to provide reiterations of a question without allotting for wait-time. This brings me to my next discovery:

I was adept at garnering high levels of participation during lessons but the same issue of reaching every child plagued my practice and so evaluators pushed me to consider ways to invite more learners into the fray. I turned to the videotape and made the following two revelations:

1. I was usually standing in one area of the classroom.
2. I often called on the same students repeatedly.

The videotape unearthed a major epiphany: I wasn't reaching all learners because I wasn't providing enough wait-time after posing a question.

I began embracing the silence of thought following a posed question. My students digested its meaning, formulated a response in their head and articulated their contribution to the class. Rates of engagement increased along with my confidence and I made a bright spot brighter because I was willing to compete with myself to improve upon an existing strength. Areas in need of improvement were moot because they didn't hinder my ability to guide students to achieve optimally. I was a pitcher with a great fastball who didn't need a Hall of Fame curveball at that moment in time.

Teams play to their strengths. If a football team has an inexperienced quarterback and a superstar running back, the coach would be wise to run the ball more often than they pass. If a basketball team has sharpshooter 3-point specialists and a lack of overall size, it'd be advisable to devise a game-plan predicated on spacing the floor and finding the open shot.

As educators we must adopt this mindset and practice a similar philosophy. Get better at what you are already good at and play to your strengths! This goes for leveraging our students' strengths in the classroom as well:

Have a chatty bunch this year? Refine their conversational skills.

Have an independent group this year? Provide more practice repetitions during lessons.

Throughout this process it's crucial that we work to our best abilities and strive to set personal records - make our bright spots brighter. Theodore Roosevelt once said that, "comparison is the thief of joy." So, the only thing we need in order to truly grow not only our proficiencies but our students' as well, is a willingness to compete with ourselves, no one else.

STEP 3: AVOID COMPARISON

STAYING WITHIN OURSELVES

Whenever you see someone at the top of their game, chances are you're seeing their life work come alive before your very eyes. As the saying goes, "it takes years to become an overnight success," and the large majority of talent who've enjoyed the throne atop their fields would agree. Throughout the journey of self-progress it's not atypical to put oneself through the ringer of comparison and while it can be used as motivation, it often rears its ugly head in destructive ways that distract from the goal of augmenting our abilities.

Let's be clear: comparison can be a force for good when looking at others as beacons of hope or positive influences. This form of comparison can be motivational as evidenced by a son telling his father, "I want to be just like you someday, dad!" or a teacher telling themselves, "I'd like to incorporate that teacher's ideas into my classroom!" A more worthwhile venture, however, is the comparison that takes place within ourselves. That is to say, seeing how far we've come or striving to beat our personal best in whatever aspect of life it may be.

Comparison is at the core of competition and competing with ourselves is the most beneficial form for enhancing our abilities and experiencing growth. Moreover, when we begin to compare ourselves to others we deprive ourselves of all the great things that make us - US!

Case in point: Musicians.

The music industry compares talent six ways from Sunday. We've all heard descriptions of new bands and musical outfits from one another: "Check them out, they're kind of a mix between ___ and ___" or "If you like ___, then you'll really like ___." All the while, musicians consistently try to be their unique selves.

Let's use the specific example of triple threat singer, songwriter, and guitarist, John Mayer; a musical superstar that knows a thing or two about being put through the comparison ringer.

A connoisseur of music and popular culture, Mayer is a prime example of a musician who was influenced by many guitarist gurus before him spanning genres and decades. Mayer's greatness can be traced back to his teenage years of practicing for hours on end to outdo himself and improve his own musical prowess for years before he was ever in the public eye.

One of his most famous moments, the live album and concert film, *Where The Light Is*, put then 30-year-old Mayer's life work on display for the world to see. Watching him during that performance, you'd be hard-pressed not to see decades of practice coming to fruition making expert level musicianship look effortless. Reaching this pinnacle was certainly not achieved by competing with or comparing himself to others, but rather confronting mental barriers and reinforcing strengths to improve his craft one step at a time.

Educators must look inward in order to achieve growth much in the same way that we preach to our students to worry about their own progress and not compare themselves with another.

Competing with ourselves by confronting mental barriers, reinforcing strengths and avoiding comparison can lead us to transformational changes that positively impacts our pedagogy and ultimately helps our learners succeed.

Competition takes a level of courage, however, and when our backs are against the wall it can be daunting to create the lasting change necessary for self-improvement. Mindset Moment #5 will chronicle how being fearless works to our benefit.

MINDSET MOMENT CHALLENGE #4!

CONFRONT YOUR MENTAL BARRIERS. TO WHAT EXTENT HAVE YOU REINFORCED AREAS OF STRENGTH?

BREAK THROUGH BARRIERS [S1 E10]

GROW YOURSELF [S2 E10]

BE FEARLESS

MINDSET
MOMENT
#5

BE FEARLESS

Fear undoubtedly plays a part in our everyday decision making especially when facing adversity. Many of us fear failure to the extent that it paralyzes us into utter inaction and we refrain from trying new things, devolving into an abyss of comfort and mediocrity rendering any chance for progress slim to none. What's more, we're either unable to recognize fear as a fleeting emotion that derives its staying power from insecurity or our inner perfectionists make us overthink and underperform, causing a vicious cycle of disappointing results until we fear failure to the degree that any effort seems futile. Becoming well acquainted with a negative headspace, a doubt in our abilities, and a low self-image equates to becoming a fearful educator who wreaks havoc on the sensitive development and progress of learners.

Here's the good news:

We can overcome the crippling fear of failure to thrive as the educators we're meant to be and who our colleagues and students deserve. We don't have to trudge through the agonizing mud of lessons falling apart and our students not progressing as intended, but can turn lessons going up in flames into lessons that fire on all cylinders.

How?

By converting failure into motivational fuel using the 3-step process of believing in our abilities, accepting outcomes and reinventing ourselves when necessary. This shift in personal ethos declutters our minds of troublesome worries and allows us to focus on achieving our best reality.

Mindset Moment #5 is a pep-talk addressing our inner voice that asks, "What if it doesn't work out?" and "What if I'm just not good enough?" and "Can I do this?" That's fear talking and wherever there is fear, there is doubt. A remedy to mitigate stressors we feel from the fear of failure and counter such destructive anxieties that inhibit our ability to perform starts with belief.

STEP 1: BELIEVE

BECOME A DOER

An undying belief in the self redefines failure as learning opportunities and converts fear into motivational fuel to overcome adversity. The nagging voice in our head, whose sole purpose is to remind us of all the possibilities that can go wrong, is 100 percent correct, and that's exactly the point: Our fears stem from the uncertainties of what may occur.

So, how do we combat the fears spawned from uncertainty of outcome?

The path of least resistance to strengthen a belief in ourselves is to take action. We become believers when we become doers and the best teacher in the world is experience.

But Andrew, I'm only beginning my career and don't have much experience.

Nonsense. Experience by definition is knowledge or skill derived from observation of or participation in events. We can be 20 years old with 100 experiences packed into 2 years or 100 years old with 2 experiences packed into 20 years. It's about doing - not about how long you've been doing, or not doing. Although we may not have "experience" in a given context, we can find applicable experiences from our lives to help solidify a belief that we can get through anything.

What if I've just failed at everything, though?

The law of probability tells us that the more we do - the more we fail but I'd revise the statement to the more we do - the more we learn how to do.

Reimagine one's first attempts - i.e. learning how to talk, walk, ride a bike, tie a shoe, how to swim (you get the point). Throughout our lives we've initially failed at so many things that we've become really good at through continuous doing, albeit I won't be performing in any swimming contests anytime soon.

So, why is everything scary until we do it?

It comes down to self-belief. Standing at the base of a mountain and seeing the summit appear far in the distance can fill us with doubt. Incremental successes add to our self-belief like water droplets filling a bucket. The more we do, the more we believe in our ability to do even more until the bucket fills up, overflows, and we've conquered the task at hand and have reached the summit ready to take on the next challenge with a strengthened belief in ourselves to achieve. Incremental success builds our self-belief and eliminates fears of the unknown. We begin to believe in ourselves to get a job done when progress is evident.

Take Formula 409's story, for example. Its two inventors certainly did not fear failure. As a matter of fact, they embraced it, invited it, and made it part of the learning process to help them reach their desired goal of creating the greatest cleaning product to hit the market. The Detroit-based inventors didn't quit nor became deterred on their 10th try.

They didn't throw in the towel on their 100th, 200th, 300th, or 400th try, either. The inventors failed 408 times before settling on the 409th solution of the cleaner and the name stuck. They're the quintessence of self-belief and converting failure into motivational fuel. They didn't fear failure but rather used it to inch closer to actualizing their vision of success.

It seems counterintuitive to embrace the prospect of failure as part of the learning process and pathway to success when it is the very thing for which we are fearful and try to avoid at all costs. Even so, first responders are trained to run towards the sound of sirens and we as lead learners in the institutions of academia must train ourselves to welcome failure as a stepping stone for growth. Using failures to our advantage desensitizes us to its crippling power and compounds incremental successes en route to accomplishing a goal, as seen with Formula 409.

Accepting failure as a valuable cornerstone of the learning process instills a level of risk-taking within our classroom of learners as well. Calling upon the influence of the famous adage, "Keep your friends close and your enemies closer," if we "keep our successes close and our failures closer," it helps us more readily accept outcomes and use them as springboards to succeed.

STEP 2: ACCEPT

CHARGE IT TO THE GAME

Suppressing negative effects we feel from the fear of failure can best be achieved through acceptance. Believing in ourselves does not always equal success, as we may fall short of our goal despite our best efforts. In this instance, it's advisable to charge it to the game and start again tomorrow.

Let's turn our attention to the Japanese term, wabi-sabi, or finding the beauty in imperfection. Wabi-sabi shifts our perspective to view failure in a different light. This may not be music to our inner perfectionist's ears, but the following depiction of wabi-sabi will illustrate its importance.

Italian restaurateur and chef of three-Michelin-star eatery, Osteria Francescana, Massimo Bottura has pushed the limits of traditional Italian cuisine. His innovative approach to stylistically plating entrees spawned from a serendipitous mistake made by one of the restaurant staffers one fateful evening.

Legend has it that a waiter dropped a dish and it splattered all over the kitchen, momentarily halting all service to the dining room. For a busy night, aiming to please and impress the masses, this setback may have pushed any driven professional over the edge. Instead of getting upset at the culinary faux pas, Bottura was inspired by the blunder and started making dishes with strategically placed smear and splatter patterns following the incident. Bottura was able to embrace the beauty in the imperfections and use it for something positive; a new style of plating at his restaurant.

Accepting outcomes lessens the negative impact that the fear of failure has on us. In fact, embracing the concept of wabi-sabi is in our best interest for rolling with the punches and finding the positive in any result.

I think we'd all rather move forward filled with optimism and confidence as opposed to debilitating fear and anxiety. "Que sera, sera" or, "whatever will be, will be" is a comforting thought and having the ability to take what's been given to us in any given scenario and pivot our energies for the good is an enormous advantage for us and an added tally mark to fear's loss column.

STEP 3: REINVENT

VERSATILITY IS OUR FRIEND

Versatility, or our ability to adapt is a key component for cutting fear at the knees. Increasing our versatility means we increase our chances of success. While the fear of failure is a formidable foe, it can motivate us to improve along with a belief in ourselves.

How can we become fearless to achieve our aspirations?

Through actualizing different iterations of ourselves.

The following quote were the words spoken by martial arts icon, Bruce Lee, during an interview amid his heyday in Hollywood:

"Empty your mind. Be formless, shapeless - like water. You put water into a cup, it becomes the cup. You put water into a bottle, it becomes the bottle. You put it in a teapot, it becomes the teapot. Now water can flow or it can crash. Be water, my friend."

Bruce Lee embodied fearlessness and his words ring true with respect to reinventing oneself and being adaptable to different situations and contexts. After being shunned by Hollywood, Lee converted the initial failure into motivational fuel by putting his renewed vigor on display in Hong Kong, ironically catching the eyes of Hollywood filmmakers.

There is unlimited power in reinventing ourselves and we often reach the pinnacle of our potential through iteration.

Spanx founder Sara Blakely is another example of successfully reinventing oneself in the face of failure.

A one time aspiring attorney, turned Disney World employee, turned door-to-door fax machine saleswoman, Blakely reinvented herself into a billionaire CEO with her hosiery creation, Spanx. Despite being turned away time and again by manufacturers at the onset, Blakely remained steadfast that her hosiery concept had legs (pun intended) and pushed through self-doubt and the fear of failure to emerge successful.

What does this have to do with teaching?

A lot.

Our profession is a very personal space and many of us fear ridicule from superiors, peers, and perhaps even students if we try embedding new techniques into our pedagogy and fall flat on our faces. This fear is universal as we often tie instructional prowess to self-worth, an unfair yet true sentiment; ask any educator, they'll likely agree this to be a pervasive mindset among the constituency.

In the best sense, we use fear for contingency planning, i.e., pre-planning checks for understanding throughout a lesson to ensure students grasp the topic or skill, preparing materials and resources to support those with misconceptions, or even dressing to impress for conferences and observations. In the worst sense, we let fear knock us off our game nearly rendering us incapable of fulfilling job requirements. From there, a mindset of inactivity becomes our fortress of solitude; we can't ever lose if we don't ever play the game, right? However, if we do not embody a fearlessness to try new things and build our skill-sets, how can we possibly expect that of our students without reeking of hypocrisy?

A common misnomer about success and failure is that they exist on opposite ends of a spectrum. Rather, they share a relationship more closely denoting that of interdependence. Failure is often a key ingredient that contributes to inevitable success because it provides us with newfound learnings and pinpoints areas of growth; invaluable takeaways from something that so many of us avoid and detest.

Any amount of success requires effort tenfold. The famous epigram credited to René Descartes, "I think, therefore I am" comes to mind when considering our fear of failure to be quite rash because many of us would agree that, "we succeed because we fail."

Being fearless and carrying on to the best of our ability takes time and effort. Converting failure into motivational fuel takes time and effort. Believing in our abilities takes time and effort. Accepting outcomes takes time and effort. Reinventing ourselves takes time and effort.

This courage to continue despite the level of difficulty is called perseverance.

MINDSET MOMENT CHALLENGE #5!

WHAT IS YOUR MOTIVATION TO KEEP GOING?

REC
00:00:01
DON'T FEAR FAILURE [S1 E3]

REC
00:00:01
WABI-SABI [S2 E8]

PERSEVERE

MINDSET
MOMENT
#6

MINDSET MOMENT #6

PERSEVERE

As educators we are tasked with sharpening students' hard skills in core content areas like reading, mathematics, and science. We're also tasked with ingraining into our students the soft skills deemed necessary for life success such as communication, creativity, and problem solving, to name a few. However, this doesn't occur through osmosis and is an arduous mission when accounting for the intangibility and nuance of enhancing students' mental acuities. The skill-building process requires a hefty dose of sticktoitiveness, more commonly referred to as perseverance, or the continued effort to achieve something despite the level of task difficulty, number of failures experienced, or opposition felt along the way.

Perseverance is the linchpin skill that helps us develop all other skills. It's acquired through the trials and tribulations of personal experience, hardship or over time through extensive efforts. The key for educators is how we cultivate within our students, a mentality to persevere.

We can all think back to times of personal disappointment and triumph, the latter being what we hope our students experience on aggregate throughout their time in academia. Rather than evoking feelings coupled with giving up such as disappointment and shame, we have a universal desire to help students feel the prideful elation of success and uphold the value of hard work through perseverance. After all, nothing is more sobering than not knowing how to help a struggling learner waving the white flag.

We've all been there.

How can educators help their students persevere when experiencing difficulties?

Mindset Moment #6 discusses strategies of support to help ourselves and others possess the mental fortitude to keep going in times of despair and difficulty. By celebrating small victories, sticking to the basics, and practicing positive self-talk we can boost a mindset of sticktoitiveness and prevent ourselves and others from giving up.

STEP 1: CELEBRATING SMALL VICTORIES

THE MOTIVATIONAL ZEST TO KEEP GOING BOILS DOWN TO PATIENCE

Celebrating small victories creates a desire to continually achieve whereas failing to recognize small successes leads to frustration and dissuades us from putting forth effort. This is one of the many reasons educational practitioners believe in positively narrating desired student behaviors and in upholding the health of professional learning communities. Celebrating small victories works as a motivational technique to uplift others to continue to exert maximum effort amid challenging circumstances.

Educators are motivators who encourage learners to build upon previous success to become their best selves. As motivators it's important that we help our learners view success as incremental and personal growth as a long-term investment.

This requires patience.

Confucius is credited with the following sentiment: "Our greatest glory is not in never falling, but in rising every time we fall."

A notable representation of perseverance are skateboarders. Taking Confucius quite literally, skateboarders fall, get back up and try again ad nauseam until they're satisfied with their level of improvement. Their sticktoitiveness and patience to succeed is second to none and something to admire. Skateboarders operate from varied skill levels yet all subscribe to the same mindset; each minuscule improvement contributes to pulling off the next great trick!

Skateboarders relentlessly practicing tricks specific to their skill level is similar to our students operating on personalized learning pathways. Students are not a monolith and require support particular to their areas of need. In order for us to help every learner be at their best, we can take a page from skateboarding culture and affix our eyes to the skill of patience.

While we may be well aware that patience is a virtue, our students are not. Overnight successes take years to accomplish and learners growing up in the age of instant gratification may find the development of perseverance to be quite challenging. Exercising patience with ourselves and others when grappling with challenging tasks illuminates the value of small successes as a cause for celebration since each minor victory brings us closer to the eventual goal.

I enjoy sharing the timeless tale of Thomas Edison inventing the lightbulb with students when highlighting patience and sticktoitiveness. After failing to invent the lightbulb 1,000 times before he actually did, Edison told a reporter, "I didn't fail 1,000 times. The lightbulb was an invention with 1,000 steps." Accounts of the tale vary but the message conveyed remains worthwhile: We're never sure how close we are to success so it's critical we don't give up, remain patient with the process, and celebrate small achievements that edge us closer to our desired outcome. A level of patience is needed to stay positive and persevere when the outlook to achieve our desired outcome is grim. Celebrating small victories is the antidote to keep going.

How can we stay patient and positive when it seems progress has eluded us?

I've always had an affinity for the following aphorism: The master has failed more times than the beginner has even tried. This captures the essence of perseverance, or the courage to continue no matter the odds. Perseverance is about never giving up and holding steadfast to the belief that we can get through anything. While this attitude appeals to our emotions, it can only carry us so far without the proper supports in place to forge ahead.

Exercising patience and positive narration in our classrooms is an excellent strategy to keep our students motivated to work through struggles. As mentors and motivators we must go beyond this initial step. This means vanilla narration like, "Great Job!" and "I love how you're working!" won't cut it for celebrating small victories because it lacks specificity. We must be explicit with our approach so as to motivate our students to replicate high level performances and proliferate their abilities.

One way to make sure we're specific in what we celebrate and aligned to supporting the achievement of goals is to anchor down to the efficiency of the basics.

STEP 2: BRINGING IT BACK TO BASICS

DOING THE SIMPLE THINGS EXCELLENTLY

"Doing the simple things excellently is the difference between professionals and amateurs."

The timbre of my coach's voice echoed throughout the empty Italian stadium as we wrapped up our final practice before a championship tournament match against Ferencvárosi TC, a professional football club from Budapest, Hungary. I was 16 years old and the wide-eyed captain of a ragtag Cinderella story team from Queens, New York.

My coach at the time, an ex-professional footballer himself, relentlessly preached being masters of simplicity. It was not uncommon for him to label a training session as "professional-grade" even though many of us didn't qualify our field basics to be anything extraordinary. Low and behold, we found ourselves a long way from the streetlights of Queens, New York, and thrust into the bright stadium lights of the global soccer community representing the United States against an international soccer power in Italy.

We suffered a heartbreaking 1-0 loss but the fact that we had gotten that far was a testament to our focus of executing the basics. You'd be hard-pressed to find any discipline that doesn't preach keeping it simple and there's a reason for that, namely because it produces the best results.

Educators can use this mentality to persevere through the demands of our day and achieve the goal of helping 100 percent of our students be successful, as stated in Mindset Moment #1. We don't have to be superheroes and do it all regardless of public perception; such pressures are gratuitous and we'd be bereft of quality educators if this were to always be the case. What we can do, however, is help our learners persevere in our classrooms and beyond by putting in place the supports necessary to help them achieve personal growth.

How can we achieve this?

Among the plethora of best practices at our fingertips nowadays, there's one practical strategy that encompasses the essence of supporting our learners to persevere: a framework I refer to as the "Core Four." Simplifying our task increases our ability to persevere and the "Core Four" keeps us on track to achieve a goal. The "Core Four" acts as bowling lane bumpers, if you will, making sure we hit our target and avoid falling into the gutter, aka giving up (I promised a friend I'd sneak in a bowling reference).

Throughout a lesson, any student at any given moment should be able to answer the following four questions:

1. What am I doing?
2. Why am I doing this?
3. How do I do it?
4. How do I know if I'm doing it well?

Being concise, clear, and informative are three ways the "Core Four" keeps it simple and ties us to basic principles. Let's take a closer look at how we can accomplish this using our percent of a number lesson example:

1. WHAT AM I DOING?

Be clear with students about the learning target and how it is being measured.

"Hi everyone! Today we're continuing our mathematics unit involving ratios and percents. By the end of this lesson, you should be able to find a percent of a number by drawing a double number line diagram."

Referencing Mindset Moment #1, this clearly states the desired future outcome for students and simplifies their target.

2. WHY AM I DOING THIS?

Sell students on the importance and relevance of the lesson to their everyday life. This is your value proposition.

"You know down the line it may be critical to compute percentages mentally and using these visuals can help you get there! I know even this morning I was online shopping and was trying my best to calculate the sales percentages in my head to get the best deals!"

This layer provides relevance to student life and gives reason to keep trying throughout the lesson.

3. HOW DO I DO IT?

Walk students through the steps/method/technique/etc.

"These are the steps to guide your thinking that you can turn to whenever you're experiencing difficulty with a given question!"

- Read problem
- What are we looking for?
- What do we know?
- Revise as a percent
- What needs to be on the double number line? Units, 0/0
- What number represents 100%?
- How many intervals to break this into? Why?
- How do we find 25 of 80? 50? 75? What is the answer?

Supporting students with concrete steps helps them break down abstract concepts into a tangible formula that alleviates stress. This layer of concreteness also pinpoints areas of struggle and helps students articulate where difficulties are being experienced throughout the process.

4. HOW DO I KNOW IF I'M DOING IT WELL AND ACHIEVING THE LEARNING TARGET?

Provide exemplars, rubrics, task cards, checklists, leveled at-bats for repetition and practice, etc.

"While you're working you may wonder if your process and answer are correct and that's normal, don't worry! Just adhere to the steps I provided you earlier and check your resource documents like our exemplar and rubric to self-assess prior to asking for help. Constantly ask yourself about our learning target: Are you finding the percent of a number by drawing a double number line? You've got this!"

Remember: we're teaching a skill, not an activity. Keeping students skill focused and not necessarily driven to complete an assignment, but motivated to learn a skill is at the core of persevering. It's not about completion but about how well we have completed whatever it is that we're working on.

Do the simple things excellently.

The "Core Four" strategy has shaped the way in which I conduct pre-observation conferences with teachers. I believe we're doing an amazing job of providing a quality education when our instructional plans satisfy the following questions:

1. What is the objective of your lesson?
2. How do you plan to differentiate instruction?
3. How will you check for understanding during the lesson?
4. How will you assess if the students have achieved the goal of the lesson?

Everyone's "difficult" is different; one person's impossible is another person's easy. The "Core Four" serves as a baseline prioritizing simplicity and retaining significance in order to support students in attaining the desired future outcome. In other words, this framework helps all students persevere during challenging academic practice.

Speaking of practice, let's address the following:

The saying, "practice makes perfect" is misleading. Consider shooting basketball free throws. No matter your level of basketball IQ or ability, we could go outside right now and shoot 1,000 free throws but if we're not focusing on the simple details, we're just going to get really good at shooting free throws the wrong way. This would be a lot of wasted effort and practice that's not making us perfect.

Think of it this way: it's better for us to shoot ten free throws perfectly than to shoot 1,000 incorrectly. Focusing on doing the simple things excellently builds competencies and organically trains us to persevere by upholding an expectation of ourselves; a critical mindset to instill in our students who rush through material making careless mistakes. Preaching quality over quantity yields better student output every time and consistent quality takes perseverance.

Do the simple things excellently.

Bringing it back to the basics may suffice with respect to supporting student thinking and reinforcing a mindset to persevere but can lack the motivational aspects to keep going. Adding the human element of positive self-talk enables our inner voice to tell us, "I can do this!"

STEP 3: POSITIVE SELF-TALK

ENCOURAGING OURSELVES TO PERSEVERE

"I think I can" is one of the most empowering statements we can tell ourselves when facing adversity. In fact, of all the success stories known to humankind it'd be difficult to pluck one out of a hat where an individual degraded themselves throughout their path to achievement. Silencing our inner doubt and encouraging ourselves is a helpful mechanism that carries us from start to finish. Positive self-talk develops our inner optimist to help us look on the bright side no matter how intimidating a challenge may appear.

The story of *The Little Engine That Could* is a great example of positive self-talk and grit, or the perseverance to achieve a goal. Without spoiling the plot, the little engine kept telling itself, "I think I can," when faced with a challenge and was ultimately able to succeed. While we can generate our own positive affirmations to help us through challenges, our students may lack this ability.

Enter educators as encouragers.

It's not easy to show up everyday and work on self-improvement yet this is the job of teachers and students, alike. One way we can make the process enjoyable is to assist our students in their pursuit of achievement and growth with positive feedback that helps develop their inner optimists. It's vital, however, that our encouraging feedback is specific to task so we don't mistake activity for achievement. Throughout the process of developing our inner optimists, it's important that we remain goal-oriented.

There's a difference between a great effort and a job well done. The following scenario illustrates the point:

At our final practice in Italy before the big game I shot the ball and it hit off the goal post creating an echo that rattled throughout the empty stadium. The jarring noise generated led one of my teammates to yell, "Wow, great shot!" I remember feeling on top of the world like I had achieved a rare feat envied by many. The exchange prompted my coach to halt practice and address the situation:

"It was a great effort - not a great shot. Great shots go in the net. Great shots help us win. For such a "great shot" we have very little to show for it. So, next time, knee over the ball - square your hips - and you'll score!"

Activity does not equate to achievement. What's most important is the fact that he provided me with specific bits of feedback to be used in the future to achieve, i.e., "next time, knee over the ball - square your hips - and you'll score!"

Instead of "I think I can" the positive self-talk phrase permeating throughout my mind was, "knee over the ball - square your hips - and you'll score!"

Positive self-talk is much more than just making ourselves feel good. It is about latching onto usable information to help pull us through the mud of hard work and bring us closer to achieving our end goal.

The real takeaway from this story is how my coach helped me develop my inner optimist with specific positive feedback. I knew I had it in me to score and even had a specific way to positively talk myself through the process. Had my coach merely agreed with my teammate and said, "Great shot!" I would have had no recourse to improve and might've even had my head in the clouds.

This is the danger of unspecific positivity. We can lead ourselves and our students astray, having strong inner optimists while achieving not very much at all.

This scenario runs rampant in classrooms. We walk around our rooms saying things like, "Good job!" and "Keep going!" which is encouraging but lacks specificity to help learners inch closer to achievement. Student A may wonder what "Good job!" means, i.e., is my teacher praising how I'm seated, the neatness of my work, my actual answer, etc?

The better alternative is to provide specific feedback to build our inner optimists with usable information, like my coach did for me. This way, we, as well as our students, can better recognize small successes, anchor efforts to basics, and encourage ourselves and others to keep going with a keen focus on the desired outcome, like skateboarders working toward the actualization of new tricks.

Our educator mindset is equally as important as our educator skill-set in order for our students to grow their capacity to persevere. Along our personal and professional paths we've had many benefactors in the form of mentors, coaches, and guides to help us develop the mental fortitude to continue despite innumerable difficulties that jeopardized our attainment of success.

It's our time to pay it forward by celebrating small victories, sticking to basics, and helping our students enhance their inner optimists with positive self-talk via specific feedback.

In order to do this, however, we must first know how to reframe. If we fail to see opportunities in every situation then we may fail to instill the qualities of determination, dedication, and stamina within our students.

MINDSET MOMENT CHALLENGE #6!

CONSIDER HOW CLOSE YOU ARE TO SUCCESS.
WHAT'S HOLDING YOU BACK?

REC

00:00:01

PRACTICE MAKES PERMANENT [S1 E6]
POSITIVE SELF-TALK [S1 E14]

REC

00:00:01

PERSEVERANCE [S2 E6]
NEVER GIVE UP [S2 E7]

REFRAME

MINDSET MOMENT #7

REFRAME

By nature human beings navigate through life accumulating experiences far and wide. Unforgettable experiences burn into our memories spanning the gamut but more often than not, we're inclined to dwell on the negatives of a situation no matter how positive an experience may be overall.

Picture this: A lesson is being executed exactly to plan and all learners are attending to tasks and on track to achieve the learning target. The class is a cognitively busy environment when an administrator walks in to see Student A flick Student B on the side of the head during partner practice and the two students begin to bicker. Instead of recalling how well the lesson was going up to that point, the teacher is likely to fixate on the quarrel between the students that their administrator witnessed and anticipate criticism.

We can all relate to this vignette in one way or another. This is negativity bias, or the phenomenon that we focus on the negatives of an experience rather than the positives. Negative bias can skew our lens and leave us ruminating on the sole unpleasant occurrence amid a sea of positive outcomes.

What if there was a way for educators to reframe their negative bias in order to see the positive in every situation?

Mindset Moment #7 puts forth a 3-part solution to shift our minds away from being prone to negativity and give more weight to elevating the positives by reframing our negative bias, seeing the opportunities in every situation and turning criticism into motivation.

STEP 1: REFRAME NEGATIVE BIAS

BE SOLUTION-ORIENTED

Negative bias drags us down and produces some alarming psychological effects we'd be better off to avoid for the sake of our mental wellness. Half the battle is being aware of our tendency to err on the side of negativity and dial into our ability to reframe, or see things through a different lens geared toward the positive.

The following personal narrative provides clarity:

I played soccer for the better part of a decade and scored too many goals to count; many being penalty kicks. While I don't remember all of them, I can amazingly recall all the penalties I missed.

Three, and I remember the details of each:

1. I was 12 years old in Valley Stream, New York competing against our cross-town rival in a league game for first place.
2. I was 14 years old in Tampa, Florida trying to advance into the final stage of an exhibition bracket.
3. I was 17 years old in Potomac, Maryland in the knockout round of a tournament.

I can also tell you exactly what happened thereafter: we lost each game and with every missed penalty came a steeper nosedive in confidence level.

I'd assuredly fail at telling you the amount of game winning goals I scored throughout my soccer career but was able to recall three instances quite readily from a rolodex of games spanning about ten years.

What does this tell us?

It's simple: The negatives frequently draw more attention than the positives.

Our brains are programmed with negative bias and this can affect our motivation to complete tasks in the future. We tend to dwell on the negatives, and yes, I still think about those missed chances as evidenced by their inclusion in this book.

So, how do we combat this?

We reframe.

Rather than fixating on the missed penalty shots it'd be more helpful to hone in on the experience gained to glean what can be done better the next time out.

Reframing our negative bias helps us transform our perspectives and attitudes. Instead of reinforcing the "misery loves company" stereotype in the teacher's lounge, we can be a positive force for others by becoming solution-oriented. This means offering energies to move beyond challenges and toward progress.

Referencing our opening vignette, it's a costly perspective to zero in on two students momentarily bickering with one another as opposed to viewing the lesson as an overall success. Perseverating on what went wrong distracts from a focus on progress and we get more bang for our buck by reflecting on what went right and how to reproduce such results. Many administrators would also notice the lesson's positives notwithstanding the incident between the two students. Instead of the teacher thinking the lesson was a failure because of a momentary hiccup, they must remember that all learners were attending to tasks and succeeding at every turn to achieve the learning target, something that is easy to forget when negativity bias enters the fray.

Reframing is a self-reflective choice aligning our headspace to positivity. We can see ourselves in the opening vignette and possibly have thought any variation of the following with respect to the two students "ruining" a lesson: Student A and B are behavioral problems. They don't enjoy school. They're not "good" students, etc.

Don't wallow in the land of such negativity. An alternative to succumbing to this temptation is to be solution-oriented and reframe.

Questions to ask ourselves might include:

- What about the lesson engaged other students during partner practice?
- How can I better engage Student A and B to work together productively?
- Should I adjust seating arrangements and switch partnerships?
- Can I approach content in a different manner to better peak their interests?

The above questions seek solutions as opposed to playing the blame game. Reframing is not so much seeing a silver lining in every condition as much as it is recognizing an alternative pathway to success. We can reframe a situation we've been dwelling on to eliminate negative bias by seeing opportunities in everything to move forward and progress with positive energy.

STEP 2: SEE OPPORTUNITIES

THINK OUTSIDE THE BOX

Seeing opportunities is more within our wheelhouse when we think outside the box. American author Regina Brett is credited with the following: "If we all threw our problems in a pile and saw everyone else's, we'd grab ours back."

"It can always be worse" is a very humbling thought and seeing opportunities in all things no matter the adverse conditions is a powerful flip of the script to help us stay positive and reframe.

I learned the value of this at the age of 6. I was diagnosed with a bone disease disrupting the blood supply to my left hip called Legg-Calve-Perthes. It's a childhood condition that I admittedly should know much more about considering it affected the entirety of my early days and molded much of my mental makeup. Legg-Calve-Perthes disease is shrouded in mystery related to its causes and affects less than 1 percent of the general population, usually more prevalent in boys.

The condition rendered me unable to walk on my own, using the assistance of crutches for nearly 6 years and undergoing physical therapy sessions 3 times a day, every single day from 1st through 6th grade. You can imagine how an active young boy's life would be blown to a million bits upon hearing the diagnosis and detailed road to recovery.

I remember sitting in the Manhattan offices of Dr. Wallace B. Lehman, the man to whom I owe a great deal. I remember my legs dangling off the examination table as his large frame knelt down to meet my eye level and deliver the news that my chances of getting drafted by the New York Rangers just got a tad slimmer (hockey was my first love).

Sparing you the technicalities, by the age of 12 I had made a full rebound and carried on with my life.

Why have I told you this?

It's the perfect example of thinking outside the box to reframe our perspective and see opportunity.

Legg-Calve-Perthes caused me years of trepidation but it also gave me many advantages, i.e., a broader perspective, wisdom beyond my years, a deep understanding of the value of hard work and perseverance, an unquenchable thirst for knowledge, and a love for the arts. For all the pain the debilitating disease caused it helped me to adopt a mindset of appreciation; something I rely on heavily to keep negativity at bay.

How did I manage to reframe instead of succumbing to a defeatist attitude when presented with a proverbial mindset fork in the road?

Suppressing the inner voice yelling, "Why me?" and amplifying my inner optimist saying, "We can get through this!" was made possible with the help of a team. I had an amazing support system surrounding me consisting of family, friends, and medical professionals that helped me reframe and see the bright side of things. I vividly remember physical therapists making the monotonous tasks fun and X-ray and MRI technicians talking me through agonizing procedures. I recall my parents encouraging me each day when I was feeling down and I appreciated my innovative doctor's smile and warmth during each visit. Every individual effort contributed to my ability to push through hardship and heal in every sense of the word. My progress and eventual triumph over Legg-Calve-Perthes is the product of everyone coming together to see opportunity in the darkest of times.

This strongly correlates to our work as educators.

No matter the intensity of demands and the amount of reasons we have to call foul, we must always see the opportunities in every situation and uplift one another when working toward common goals. We deal with the human element and aren't isolated contractors but a moving part in a much larger organism. We're each a spoke contributing to the forward movement of the wheel and together can adjust our collective lens, i.e., Student A and B aren't "bad kids," our administrators aren't "awful people," parents aren't "obstacles," and our coworkers aren't "incapable." Upholding such callous views is to submit to negative bias and become a poster-child for learned helplessness. Operating from a solution-oriented point of view and striving for progress no matter how dire a situation seems is the mark of true character. For every issue or limitation encountered, we can conjure up a work around to eclipse it and succeed; a sentiment we keep present in our students' minds frequently, mind you.

Still not convinced?

One of the more fascinating stories you'll ever hear about seeing opportunities amid damning odds is the story of the red paperclip.

Focusing on the opportunities of situations rather than the problems can be challenging amid our own negativity bias and Canadian blogger Kyle MacDonald provides us with a story of thinking outside the box and seeing opportunities we're sure not to forget.

MacDonald managed to trade one single red paperclip for a complete two story house.

Read that line again.

MacDonald accomplished this in a series of 14 trades lasting over a year's time. It's a really good example of seeing big opportunity in not so much but it paying off big time in the end. MacDonald's story of bartering success became viral to the point that he presented a TEDx Talk documenting the amazing journey.

Don't focus on problems. Think differently and see opportunities.

All of our Mindset Moments up to this point become more powerful with our ability to reframe. Seeing the opportunity in everything and seeing the potential in ourselves and others shifts our focus from what we cannot do to what we can. This is especially significant for educators working alongside children who may not yet have the ability to reframe and see opportunities within challenges.

STEP 3: TURN CRITICISM INTO MOTIVATION

BEWARE THE AMYGDALA HIJACK

Turning criticism into motivation is no walk in the park. There are different forms of criticism with each type boiling down to the identification and judgment of faults. For many, criticism equates to personal attack and defensiveness prevails, often making any offered advice to improve fall on deaf ears. However, we could learn a thing or two from the story of Austin's butterfly, a shining example of how to turn criticism into motivation.

Austin was a primary student who received feedback on his drawings and was able to use that feedback to unleash his true potential and improve his drawings over time. He used the criticism to depict a more accurate representation of a butterfly over a series of drafts resulting in a polished finished product.

Austin was able to avoid what's called an amygdala hijack, which is when our brain triggers certain anxieties to make us feel threatened; the exact response we want to avoid for ourselves and our students. Shifting our mindset to use criticism as motivation to improve our abilities pays dividends in the form of maintaining a positive headspace and enabling us to progress in our endeavors.

Why is this a significant practice for educators to employ?

We're susceptible to being blinded by our own emotions. An example of this is a film editing technique called the Kuleshov effect, a mental phenomenon where viewers derive more meaning from sequential shots than is really there. A man smiling followed by a shot of a dog leads us to believe the man must be smiling at or because of seeing the dog, which may not be the case at all. The Kuleshov effect was meant to show the power of film editing but it proves something much more powerful: we fill in the blanks and see what we want to see.

Following this logic, we believe the stories we tell ourselves.

My lesson was horrible because my administrator saw two students off task versus thinking about all the learners attending to task and achieving the learning target.

I'm awful at soccer because I missed a penalty shot versus considering all the goals I scored to put my team in a position to be successful.

Legg-Calve-Perthes disease ruined my childhood versus realizing the gifts it actually bestowed upon me.

A red paperclip is worthless versus contemplating who might be in need of one.

I'm terrible at drawing butterflies versus using feedback to improve my ability to draw butterflies.

Mindset Moment #7 helps us reframe our thinking for a better tomorrow. At the end of the day we are storytellers. We are the entrusted gatekeepers to dispense knowledge into young minds and disseminate valuable learnings through the art of story. What we tell ourselves and others has a profound and lasting impact on the development of our positive lens through which we see the world and the vast opportunities within our grasp.

MINDSET MOMENT CHALLENGE #7!

HOW CAN YOU TURN CRITICISM INTO MOTIVATION AND PROBLEMS INTO OPPORTUNITIES?

REC

00:00:01

SEE OPPORTUNITIES [S1 E12]
CRITICISM TO MOTIVATION [S1 E15]

REC

00:00:01

REFRAME NEGATIVE BIAS [S2 E11]

BE AUTHENTIC

Living out our best realities comes down to one thing: being ourselves. Pretending to be something other than what we truly are robs us and the world of the wonderful gifts we have to offer. Achieving our best self proves difficult amid lingering issues of confidence or a lack of knowhow, though. What's more, pressures stemming from internal ambitions or external expectations can leave us feeling inadequate, further deteriorating our self-worth and self-image swaying us to lean toward disenguinity and a lack of personal connection; the lifeblood of educators.

How can we achieve our best self to succeed as lead learners in the face of such challenges?

Mindset Moment #8 serves as a friendly reminder to be ourselves by focusing on the importance of authenticity to educator practice. Within this Mindset Moment are 3 ways of finding ourselves while navigating the world of education: discovering our voice, understanding ourselves and fulfilling our potential. In order to be a great teacher we must be great learners and that starts with the studying of ourselves.

STEP 1: DISCOVERING OUR VOICE

PUT PERSONALITY FIRST

Prior to entering the educational arena I was an Accounting major at Hofstra University's Zarb School of Business in Long

Island, New York. I assumed the role after taking the sage advice of an academic advisor who recognized the aspirations of a sophomore athlete and provided a recession proof profession to serve as a plan B barring any shortcomings along the road to the big leagues.

Long story short: I hated it. I hated it so much in fact that I graduated early with a B.B.A in Accounting just to rid myself of the nuisance getting in the way of my athletic dreams.

Life humbled me and I began working as an Accountant in Tribeca, Manhattan, a hip area lined with trendy shops and known for its cobblestone streets (if you need restaurant recommendations - I'm your guy). For many young college graduates it was a dream position and so I worked on business expense reports and tax forms by day while training youth soccer teams by night (the rite of passage of any former athlete). It wasn't long before I looked forward to my evenings of helping kids more than my day job of pushing corporate papers and made the switch to the world of education to feel at home.

What does this have to do with authenticity helping educators' pedagogical practices?

In the business world they have a saying that goes like this:

"People buy your personality before they buy what you're selling."

As educators we can relate by substituting people with our students and what we're selling with our academic content a la the following:

"Kids invest in academic content when they're invested in their teacher."

Kids become invested in us as mentors when we connect and build genuine relationships. I believe this to be true and our students can only know who we are if we're uplifting our voice and letting our personalities shine through our instructional practice.

Be yourself.

Ironically, this mindset is easily forgotten when we struggle to garner high levels of student engagement. So, we borrow here and take there and purchase from over here and collect from over there like chickens without their heads forgetting the cardinal rule of educating our youth: Teacher energies beget student energies and authenticity begets engagement.

Previous Mindset Moments have covered the energies we bring to our environment and children have the superpower of detecting disingenuity time and again.

How does being our authentic selves translate to improved student engagement?

Finding our footing and discovering our voice is daunting to say the least. Along the journey we craft elaborate lessons with bells and whistles and intricate behavioral management systems to enhance student compliance in order to cover the content dictated to us via pacing guides, curriculum maps, and the like. We expect children to enter our classrooms as willing recipients ready to absorb information and move on to the next topic. When we've missed the mark we feel pressure to work even harder to deliver Academy Award winning performances to the point of desperately wishing our students are remotely entertained enough to care in the slightest way. Before long we're aspiring Broadway performers in front of disinterested audiences, resulting in us at a loss and scrambling for more cheap resources to purchase.

We've all gone down this path and it never ends with us feeling better about ourselves or our practice.

Remember: It's our job to transform students from obedient and compliant recipients of information into engaged and willing participants of acquiring new skills.

The best way to accomplish the transition is to be ourselves.

Educators as a nexus offer quality in uniqueness. Our diversity as it pertains to self and skill is what upholds our professional cache as a collective. Our students are not a monolith nor are we as their teachers and therein lies our strength as individuals contributing to a quality educational experience overall; our own unique personality and voice.

"I don't want to be the next Michael Jordan, I only want to be Kobe Bryant." These words uttered by the late, great basketball star, Kobe Bryant are conspicuous to the point:

Being our best self means understanding how to use our unique abilities to help our learners thrive in the classroom and beyond. The teacher down the hall may be the best form of professional development, but what works for them and their style may not work for someone else. Differentiating for each of our learners and not ourselves is unwise. After all, being our best self encourages them to be theirs.

Personal connection drives engagement and reeling students in with authenticity leads to students excited to enter our classrooms and sad to leave.

Living out this reality is natural for some but takes a great deal of work for others and becoming a trusted lead learner comes with an enhanced understanding of the self.

STEP 2: UNDERSTANDING OURSELVES

WORK FOR IT

When I was a kid I loved reading the book, *It's Not Easy Being A Bunny* by Marilyn Sadler. The story centered around a protagonist, PJ Funny Bunny, who wasn't happy being himself; a measly bunny. This feeling of self-discontent led him to travel far and wide to fit in with other animal groups only to discover that being a bunny had its advantages too! The payoff of Sadler's book was to be yourself and stop trying to be something that you're not. PJ Funny Bunny was only able to discover this after many rounds of trying new things, however. Through various experiences, he finally came to appreciate his own set of skills as a bunny.

Here's the deal: being at our best takes work.

Remember: students feed off our energies. If we're not being our best selves - they won't be either.

Educators carry the privilege of mentorship. Our students spend more time with us than their families on aggregate. Choosing not to be ourselves means to sacrifice the gift of educating beyond core content. For example, through personal connection we help students understand social cues and build their social awareness. These genuine interactions prepare learners for different social scenarios, i.e., most of us wouldn't dare act the same way with our grandmother at Sunday dinner the way we would with our boss in a conference room or best friend on a Friday night. Being genuine and breaking down boundaries is the core of relationship building and only made possible through authenticity. Easier said than done.

Why is it so hard for us to be ourselves?

It takes courage to let our guard down and feel vulnerable.

Business magnate Henry Ford is quoted with the following:

"Whether you think you can, or think you can't, you're right."

There's a term called imposter syndrome that essentially means we constantly doubt ourselves and our abilities. Even today we'll have anywhere from 12,000 to 60,000 thoughts bouncing around our minds, 80% of which will be negative. Even so, if we change the way we think, we can change the way we feel, and then change what we do.

What's most important is to understand that our abilities are needed to help young minds grow. We're probably not the first to think of a given strategy but our brand of execution may be the best to ignite curiosity or provide a lightbulb moment bringing our students closer to newfound learnings. Understanding ourselves means coming to the realization that we're one of one and wield power as lead learners to help guide our students in unique ways. Athletes have played before athletes, musicians have composed before musicians, actors have performed before actors, and teachers have taught before teachers. We differentiate both process and product for students to improve their skills; affording ourselves the same opportunity by doing it our way takes work but continually improves our craft.

STEP 3: FULFILLING OUR POTENTIAL

BE RESOURCEFUL

As we've progressed you may have thought the following:

I'm already self-aware, I understand who I am, and I've peaked and can't improve myself anymore.

Not so fast.

Being resourceful and subscribing to the approach that we can adapt and overcome is a key layer to actualizing our best self.

The following anecdote pays homage to a man who showed me time and again how to stretch one's personal limits and fulfill potential; my father.

I was around 7 years old when my family went to a local entertainment center geared for kids, named Fun Station. Fun Station was the type of neighborhood destination where upon opening the front doors you're smacked in the face with the overwhelming smell of buttered popcorn, clamouring laughs of rambunctious children and dizzying lights of rides and games. It was a run of the mill type of place where kids reigned supreme and a parent's love and tolerance for their children was tested.

I remember like it was yesterday entering the haven and feasting my eyes upon a gigantic velcro wall where kids wearing a special velcro suit were launched and stuck ten or more feet above the ground. I'll spare myself the embarrassment and simply say; I very strongly urged my father to let me get in line and be launched against the wall. After quite the deliberation he finally acquiesced and we waited in the long line together only to discover I was too small for the suit. I was as dejected as could be but my father had an idea! After a brief discussion with the worker operating the station, both turned to face me with warm smiles. Within the blink of an eye, my father took off his belt, wrapped it around the oversized suit and I was good to go and happily being launched out of a cannon and splat onto a wall of velcro.

My father's resourcefulness and innovative Macgyver-like maneuver was not an on the spot one-off. His spur of the moment ability to generate such an idea was the product of a certain way of thinking. Emigrating from a home in Spain with dirt floors and no running water or electricity to the big city lights of Manhattan during his childhood contributed to a mindset of adapting and overcoming the challenges of a situation. His resourcefulness was spawned from need and ingrained into his being over time. He understood how to do more with less and fulfill his potential to become successful and impart that grit to his children for them to reach their full potential.

We must bring this attitude into our teaching.

We don't need purchased curriculums or the best equipment in order for us to be master teachers. We need ourselves to be at our best and thinking on our feet. Problems arise the likes of which we've never seen and we must be ready to handle them and move forward giving our learners the best chance to succeed. By pushing ourselves to fulfill our potential, we become able to adapt and overcome any conditions, making us much better instructors of young minds.

Ultimately, we're at our best when we achieve a level of authenticity to connect with others and let our uniqueness shine. By discovering our own voice, understanding ourselves and fulfilling our potential, the probability of our students and those around us achieving the same increases exponentially.

MINDSET MOMENT CHALLENGE #8!

ARE YOU BEING THE BEST VERSION OF YOURSELF OR ARE YOU TRYING TO BE SOMEONE ELSE?

● REC

00:00:01

YOU CAN [S1 E4]
BE YOURSELF [S1 E5]

POSITION

MINDSET
MOMENT
#9

POSITION

There's a certain duality educators balance as it relates to being experts in the field and professional learners at the same time. The allure of complacency becomes quite enticing after years of experience and seeing it all. Somewhere between the excitement to begin teaching and the gratification of completing such a rewarding career, we can forget to practice what we preach; lifelong learning.

"Ancora imparo" is an Italian phrase meaning, "Still, I am learning." I'm not Italian nor do I speak it; I'm merely skilled in the intricate art of Googling and many attribute the phrase to the Renaissance artist, Michelangelo.

Why is this significant for us as educators?

Being a master of any craft means being committed to lifelong learning. The Renaissance artist who possessed a wide array of talents apparently uttered the words while in his late 80's - far from being a spring chicken, yet still ripe and ready to learn - a perspective worthy of a closer look.

So, we consider:

How can educators continually position themselves as learners?

Mindset Moment #9 dives into a 3-pronged method to help us maintain a beginner's mindset and continually position ourselves as learners via the following: staying hungry by getting a coach, staying curious by going beyond our initial idea, and staying open-minded by remaining a sponge.

STEP 1: STAY HUNGRY

GETTING A COACH

Attaining success is one thing but maintaining it and continuing to push ourselves forward is an entirely different animal altogether. It's difficult to position ourselves as learners when we've achieved highly because of ego, or our sense of self-importance. In many cases we've built up such gumption fending for ourselves and figuring it out for so long that the toxicity of, "I know better than anyone" seeps in and we forget what we signed up for; lifelong learning.

How do we stay hungry to achieve and how do we improve our craft to become great?

We get a coach.

A coach is a set of external eyes and ears informing us how to stay atop our own personal leaderboard. The work of a coach is not rooted in persuasion but rather data-driven conversations with the purpose to help us uphold and actualize the vision of success. Coaching is a meeting of the minds through reflective conversations where the best idea to achieve a goal wins.

Great talents the world over have enlisted the help of coaches from sports stars to musicians to surgeons to CEOs of Fortune 500 corporations. Positioning ourselves as learners means humbling our ego and seeking the advice of others to continually achieve. It's immensely difficult to see ourselves as others see us and coaches provide perspective with the soul of improvement; feedback.

Educators in general are a severely under-coached bunch and because of this we've forgotten how to perform the backbone skill of our very livelihood: learn! If we want to get better at getting better we must learn and in order to learn we can't hide behind a dishonest veneer of expertise.

Let's face the hard truth of our lack of coaching by talking numbers:

The standard length of a school year is about 180 days. Generally speaking there are 6 class periods a day, each lasting 45 minutes in duration. I'm no longer an accountant but that's roughly 200 minutes of instruction per day.

200 minutes of instruction per day X 180 days of school = 36,000 instructional minutes in a school year.

What does this mean?

If teachers are observed twice in an academic year for a total of 90 instructional minutes that means 0.2% of their instruction was observed.

Here's the payoff: 98.8% of the teacher's instruction was not observed. We can agree that 0.2% is an insufficient amount of time to enjoy a cup of coffee let alone build a trusted relationship with a coach and receive worthwhile feedback to improve our craft.

Staying hungry to achieve means keeping our students' best interests at heart and that means remembering what it's like to be a learner. Through collaboration and open dialogue with a coach we can revisit this practice and be held in the same esteem as physicians, pilots, architects, and nurses, to name a few. To do anything less than to achieve the vision of success is unprofessional. In order to keep our head in the game, however, we must allow our curiosity to flourish!

STEP 2: STAY CURIOUS

GOING BEYOND OUR INITIAL IDEA

Educators as lifelong learners are pursuers of new information. We don't settle. We are pioneers of innovation in order to get the best student outcomes.

But, what's the best way to come up with really good ideas?

It's simply just to generate a lot of ideas. Inventors are professional idea generators and make a lot of discoveries by accident.

Here's an example near and dear to all educator hearts out there: the post-it note.

The inventor of the post-it note failed to create a really strong adhesive but realized by adding a small piece of paper to the equation it could be stuck to things and pulled off quite easily without leaving a mark. Remaining inquisitive paid off as the post-it note has become a pillar in the supplies index of professionals and students ever since.

Sometimes the best discoveries happen just because we keep pushing ourselves to go beyond our initial idea.

Another example of going beyond our initial idea to achieve greatness is a staple of my childhood; the Super Soaker.

Dr. Lonnie Johnson, a NASA scientist credited with over 100 patents, is responsible for creating the water guns that ruled our childhoods and incensed many an older sister (I know from experience). Initially setting out to create a green alternative to the use of Freon by experimenting with water pumps, Johnson seized the opportunity for something different altogether and the rest is history.

As educational practitioners we can sometimes hit a wall for how to best help our learners and positioning ourselves to go beyond our initial inclinations to help our students succeed is of the utmost importance. We push our students to remain curiously invested in content and affording ourselves the same level of encouragement is transformational to our practice.

STEP 3: STAY OPEN-MINDED

REMAINING A SPONGE

You've done it and seen it all ten times over. I get it and it's easy to adopt this frame of mind but thinking we know it all sullies the integrity of our practice and puts our learners in jeopardy. The fact remains, we don't know it all. Our world is ever-changing and adapting to new ways of helping our youth thrive under up to the minute conditions, the likes of which we may not yet be aware, helps us maintain a learner's approach.

What do all learners love doing?

They satisfy their quest for knowledge by reading.

Suffering from abibliophobia, or the fear of running out of things to read, is arguably a good quality for an educator to possess.

But Andrew, where do I start?

I'll be completely honest: I disliked reading as a kid until I discovered *Call It Courage* by Armstrong Sperry; a story about a boy essentially scared of the sea, and at the time I shared that fear and was captivated and transformed into the voracious bookworm I still am today.

Finding material that speaks to our specific areas of interest for growth is paramount for helping our learners; wherever we improve, so too do they. In many instances, we don't know what we don't know, and simply picking up a book can open our eyes to different possibilities or spawn an idea to incorporate into our practice to benefit our community of learners.

Stay open-minded by being a sponge. Take in any and all information and turnkey to fit the needs of you and your learners. Perhaps the most important part is getting started, however.

Enter motivational speaker Melanie Robbins' 5 Second Rule. Not to be confused with picking up food off the floor within 5 seconds preserving its edibility, Robbins' 5 Second Rule pertains to the secret of achieving our goals: taking action. More specifically, taking action within 5 seconds. She proposes that we must decide to do something within 5 seconds or our brain will talk us out of it.

Let's practice by deciding to read on below within the next 5 seconds:

Being a master teacher means being a master learner. With this comes the acceptance that there is always more learning and growth to be had. It means practicing what we preach to our students and understanding that the journey is the destination. It means balancing the duality of our existence as experts of our content areas and learners of our craft. It means positioning ourselves as learners. Always.

MINDSET MOMENT CHALLENGE #9!

HOW DO YOU MAINTAIN A LEARNER'S APPROACH?

STAY CURIOUS [S1 E13]

READ MORE [S2 E5]
STAY HUNGRY [S2 E9]

FOLLOW THROUGH

MINDSET
MOMENT
#10

FOLLOW THROUGH

Our conversation comes to a close with an impassioned plea to stay the course from me to you:

It's not everyday that we accomplish goals and achieve milestones to cap off tremendous efforts and if you've made it this far I know what you're thinking: I've tried and trying hasn't been good enough. It's true that the frequency at which we incur defeat can leave our spirit uninspired and our will in tatters. It's also true that when many of us meet resistance we shy away from our dreams not fully understanding that with exceptional ideas come exceptional challenges that demand exceptional efforts.

Enter resilience.

Resilience, or the ability to recover from and adjust to setbacks and keep going in the face of difficulty, is the name of the game. Mindset Moments sow the seeds of success only when paired with the resilience to follow through.

Consider the following:

What is one thing you always wanted to be great at?
Did you attain the level of greatness for which you set out to achieve?
- If yes, what made you able to accomplish such greatness?
- If no, what hampered your ability to succeed in your endeavor?

Resilience is the reason we succeed or fail. It's that simple.

If it's so simple then why isn't it so easy?

Negativity from naysayers, nonbelievers, or those within our inner circle erodes our will, clouds our focus, and drags us further away from our desired future. It's incumbent upon us to repel negativity and execute our goals in spite of adversity and negative influences.

Many of our undertakings spawn from the initial thought, "I can do it" or even, "I can do it better." Executing such thoughts takes hard work and dedication over long periods of time, however, and in the event we fall short of achieving goals, it's tempting to chalk it up to bad luck or misfortune forgetting that we're in control of our own destiny.

How can educators finish strong and remain undeterred by adversity?

We repel negativity with the resilience to follow through.

A fun example to mull over and strive towards: Ducks.

Although not the fiercest of the animal kingdom, they're perhaps one of the most resilient. Let me explain: Ducks' feathers are coated with an oil that keeps them warm in freezing cold temperatures and dry in water. Their feathers are water repellent; ergo, water droplets quite literally roll off of ducks' backs.

What's the takeaway?

Envision the following: you're having a great day when something puts you in a foul mood and you can't recover. We can fix that by being more like a duck and letting negativity roll off of our backs just like water. How we react to challenges is within our control and I urge you to consider the steps in this book when goal setting.

Mindset Moments provide us with a roadmap of perspective keeping our lens focused on turning possibilities into realities. Following through and finishing strong makes it all feasible.

Stay the course by repelling negativity like a duck's feathers repel water.

Create a vision of success and contribute to its actualization by anchoring actions to ideas and remaining cognizant of the impact they carry to inspire yourself and others. Compete to be better and be fearless in the face of adversity to persevere and flex your muscles of resilience throughout the process to reframe every situation into one of immense opportunity and maintain a learner's approach.

We fail because we lack the resilience to repel negativity and follow through.

The Hare and the Tortoise is a classic Aesop Fable that puts this in perspective quite nicely. The overconfident and speedy Hare was amused at the notion of racing the tortoise, going so far as ridiculing the latter for being slow and wanting to prove itself a winner in the David vs. Goliath type scenario. In the end, slow and steady won the race despite the fact that the Hare had a pretty good start. The tortoise showed a resilience to keep going while facing steep odds.

Here's the gist: It's never about how we start - it's about how we finish.

MINDSET MOMENT CHALLENGE #10!

REPEL NEGATIVITY WITH THE RESILIENCE TO FOLLOW THROUGH.

FINISH STRONG [S1 E8]
SECRET TO SUCCESS [S1 E11]

REPEL NEGATIVITY [S2 E2]
DO WHAT MAKES YOU HAPPY [S2 E3]

A FINAL THOUGHT

Mindset Moments are a methodical framework to keep us moving forward not thinking about our limitations but rather concentrating on what we can do, like the tortoise.

Roman philosopher Seneca offers the following: "Luck is what happens when preparation meets opportunity."

Preparation. Opportunity. Luck. In that order. These things are not ethereal in nature but quite tangible with a bit of gusto and a touch of zeal added to the mix. They also share one major trait in common; they create a pipeline for perennial success in the face of any hurdle.

We are the meticulous curators of every pathway we walk upon and are much more capable and in control of our fate than we often realize.

Success is a mindset and good things happen when we push through negativity and continue to work hard. The universe has an unbelievable way of handsomely rewarding us for the positive energies we outwardly extend. So, have the audacity to believe in yourself and go grab your reward.

Think about it. I'll see you later.

FRAMEWORK

VISUALIZE

ISSUE: How can educators visualize success in order to attain their desired future?

SOLUTION:
1. Vision
2. Honesty
3. Planning

CHALLENGE: Define what success looks like to you and consider the preparations needed in order to attain it.

CONTRIBUTE

ISSUE: How can educators contribute something positive to help others and themselves be successful?

SOLUTION:
1. Think Proactively
2. Demonstrate Value
3. Practice Empathy

CHALLENGE: What energies are you exuding and how are they contributing something positive to help others and yourself be successful?

REPRESENT

ISSUE: How can educators motivate others to be their best at all times?

SOLUTION:
1. Anchor actions to an idea
2. Align actions to impact
3. Inspire others through action

CHALLENGE: Who do you represent outside of yourself and how does your attitude impact them?

COMPETE

ISSUE: How can educators continually augment their personal and professional growth?

SOLUTION:
1. Confront mental barriers
2. Reinforce areas of strength
3. Avoid comparison

CHALLENGE: Confront your mental barriers. To what extent have you reinforced areas of strength?

BE FEARLESS

ISSUE: How can educators quell the fear of failure and thrive as lead learners?

SOLUTION:
1. Believe
2. Accept
3. Reinvent

CHALLENGE: What is your motivation to keep going?

PERSEVERE

ISSUE: How can educators help their students persevere when experiencing difficulties?

SOLUTION:
1. Celebrate small victories
2. Bring it back to basics
3. Positive self-talk

CHALLENGE: Consider how close you are to success. What's holding you back?

REFRAME

ISSUE: How can educators reframe negative bias in order to see the positive in every situation?

SOLUTION:
1. Reframe negative bias
2. See opportunities
3. Turn criticism into motivation

CHALLENGE: How can you turn criticism into motivation and problems into opportunities?

BE AUTHENTIC

ISSUE: How can educators achieve their best self to succeed as lead learners?

SOLUTION:
1. Discovering personal voice
2. Understanding the self
3. Fulfilling potential via resourcefulness

CHALLENGE: Are you being the best version of yourself or are you trying to be someone else?

POSITION

ISSUE: How can educators continually position themselves as learners?

SOLUTION:
1. Stay Hungry
2. Stay Curious
3. Stay Open-minded

CHALLENGE: How do you maintain a learner's approach?

FOLLOW THROUGH

ISSUE: How can educators finish strong and remain undeterred by adversity?

SOLUTION:
1. Be Resilient

CHALLENGE: Repel negativity with the resilience to follow through.

REFERENCES

1. Stryker, L. (n.d.). *Emeritus College Journal - ASU*. Meditation and the Mind. Retrieved August 8, 2020, from https://emerituscollege.asu.edu/sites/default/files/ecdw/EVoice10/meditation_and_mind.html

2. Racco, M. (2018, May 18). IKEA conducts bullying experiment on plants — the results are shocking. Global News. https://globalnews.ca/news/4217594/bully-a-plant-ikea/

3. Hoomans, J. (2015, March 20). *35,000 Decisions: The Great Choices of Strategic Leaders*. Roberts Wesleyan College. https://go.roberts.edu/leadingedge/the-great-choices-of-strategic-leaders

4. Bloom, S. G. (2005, September 1). *Lesson of a Lifetime*. Smithsonian Magazine. https://www.smithsonianmag.com/science-nature/lesson-of-a-lifetime-72754306/

5. Lewis, M. (2020, May 7). *Whatever Happened to Former USMNT Captain Mike Windischmann?* U.S. Soccer Federation. https://www.ussoccer.com/stories/2020/05/whatever-happened-to-former-usmnt-captain-mike-windischmann

6. Ingle, S. (2018, March 5). *Roger Bannister, a gentleman who almost didn't run race that defined him*. The Guardian. https://www.theguardian.com/sport/2018/mar/04/roger-bannister-gentleman-almost-never-ran-race-defined-him

7. Taylor, B. (2018, April 10). *What Breaking the 4-Minute Mile Taught Us About the Limits of Conventional Thinking*. Harvard Business Review. https://hbr.org/2018/03/what-breaking-the-4-minute-mile-taught-us-about-the-limits-of-conventional-thinking

8. Myers, C. (2017, October 6). *The 40% Rule: The Simple Secret To Success*. Forbes. https://www.forbes.com/sites/chrismyers/2017/10/06/the-40-rule-the-simple-secret-to-success/?sh=7974d66d5cdd

9. Windley, A. (2019, May 19). *Retrospective | John Mayer Shows Where the Light Is*. HeadStuff. https://www.headstuff.org/entertainment/music/retrospective-john-mayer-light/

10. Click Americana. (2020, February 12). *Where did vintage brand names like 7-Up, Formula 409 & WD-40 come from?* https://clickamericana.com/topics/discoveries-inventions/where-did-vintage-brand-names-like-7-up-formula-409-wd-40-come-from

11. Lawrence, R. G. (2001, September). *Wabi-Sabi: The Art Of Imperfection.* Utne. https://www.utne.com/mind-and-body/wabi-sabi

12. Gino, F. (2018). Rebel Talent: Why It Pays To Break The Rules At Work And In Life (1st ed.). Dey Street Books.

13. Mosley, T., & Hagan, A. (2020, June 4). "Be Water" Explores Life And Legacy Of Martial Arts Star Bruce Lee | Here & Now. WBUR.Org. https://www.wbur.org/hereandnow/2020/06/04/bruce-lee-be-water-espn

14. Reporter, S. (2018, July 25). *How Bruce Lee classic quote 'be water' from fictional US TV series came to be attributed to him.* South China Morning Post. https://www.scmp.com/culture/film-tv/article/2155586/how-bruce-lee-classic-quote-be-water-fictional-us-tv-series-came-be

15. Bikoff, M. L. (2017, December 13). *The Uplifter: How Spanx CEO Sara Blakely became one of the most inspirational women in business.* Atlanta Magazine. https://www.atlantamagazine.com/style/uplifter-how-spanx-ceo-sara-blakely-became-one-of-the-most-inspirational-women-in-business/

16. Bellis, M. (2019, March 16). *The Inventors Who Worked on the Lightbulb Besides Edison.* ThoughtCo. https://www.thoughtco.com/who-invented-the-lightbulb-1991698

17. Piper, W., Santat, D., & Parton, D. (2020). The Little Engine That Could: 90th Anniversary Edition (Illustrated ed.). Grosset & Dunlap.

18. Loranger, H. (2016, October 23). *The Negativity Bias in User Experience.* Nielsen Norman Group. https://www.nngroup.com/articles/negativity-bias-ux/

19. *Perthes Disease - Legg-Calve-Perthes - OrthoInfo - AAOS.* (n.d.). Perthes Disease. Retrieved January 7, 2021, from https://orthoinfo.aaos.org/en/diseases--conditions/perthes-disease

20. *BBC NEWS | Technology | Man turns paper clip into house.* (2006, July 11). Man Turns Paper Clip into House. http://news.bbc.co.uk/2/hi/technology/5167388.stm

21. TEDx Talks. (2015, November 20). What if you could trade a paperclip for a house? | Kyle MacDonald | TEDxVienna. YouTube. https://www.youtube.com/watch?v=8s3bdVxuFBs

22. El Education. (n.d.). *Austin's Butterfly | EL Education*. https://eleducation.org/resources/austins-butterfly

23. Mobbs, D., Weiskopf, N., Lau, H. C., Featherstone, E., Dolan, R. J., & Frith, C. D. (2006). The Kuleshov Effect: the influence of contextual framing on emotional attributions. *Social Cognitive and Affective Neuroscience, 1*(2), 95–106. https://doi.org/10.1093/scan/nsl014

24. Ury, W. (2016). Getting to Yes with Yourself: How to Get What You Truly Want (Reprint ed.). HarperOne.

25. Sadler, M., & Bollen, R. (1983). *It's Not Easy Being a Bunny (Beginner Books(R))* (Illustrated ed.). Random House Books for Young Readers.

26. Stik2It. (2016, September 20). *The History of Post-it Notes: The Accidents That Led to the Invention of the Sticky Note [INFOGRAPHIC]*. Stik2it.Com. https://www.stik2it.com/blog/the-history-of-postit-notes-the-accidents-that-led-to-the-invention-of-the-sticky-note-infographic/

27. Shereshewsky, T. G. A. B. (2020, August 15). *How a NASA Scientist Accidentally Invented the Super Soaker*. CNN. https://edition.cnn.com/2020/08/15/us/super-soaker-lonnie-johnson-great-big-story-trnd/index.html

28. Robbins, M. (2018, March 28). *How to stop screwing yourself over*. TED Talks. https://www.ted.com/talks/mel_robbins_how_to_stop_screwing_yourself_over

29. Sperry, A. (1990). *Call It Courage* (Reprint ed.). Aladdin.

30. Cassidy, J. (2020, August 18). *What Actually Makes Water Roll Off a Duck's Back?* KQED. https://www.kqed.org/science/1968261/what-actually-makes-water-roll-off-a-ducks-back

31. *The Hare and The Tortoise*. (2020, October 5). Fables of Aesop. https://fablesofaesop.com/the-hare-and-the-tortoise.html

ABOUT THE AUTHOR

ANDREW J. CANLÉ is an assistant principal, district wellness coordinator, and doctoral student from the New York Metropolitan area helping kids cultivate a positive mindset through weekly focus questions on his YouTube show, *EDUCanle Presents Mindset Moment of the Week*. Andrew's writing has been featured in such publications as *The Marshall Memo, Edutopia, MiddleWeb, DisruptED TV Magazine* and the *EDCamp Foundation*. He previously served in the capacities of sixth-grade level chair, general education classroom teacher and AIS Academy instructional coach. Andrew graduated from Hofstra University with a B.B.A. in accounting and a M.S.Ed. in elementary education for grades 1 through 6. He completed his advanced certificate in educational leadership and administration at the College of St. Rose and is currently enrolled in Hofstra University's doctoral program for educational and policy leadership with a focus on game-based interventions and student social competence. Andrew is a district certified administrator who is passionate about helping educators succeed in transforming the lives of all children and enjoys connecting with others via social media to help them overcome adversities and build resilience.

CODE BREAKER INC.

CONSULTING

To learn more about **ANDREW J. CANLÉ** or to book him for a visit to your school, district, or event, visit www.codebreakeredu.com

INSPIRE · INNOVATE

LEAD · TEACH · LEARN

CODE BREAKER LEADERSHIP SERIES

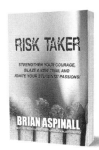

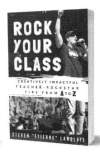

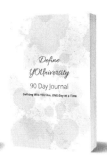

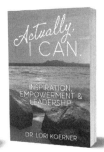

CODE BREAKER KID COLLECTION

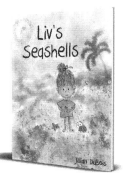
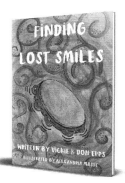

www.codebreakeredu.com

Made in the USA
Middletown, DE
29 July 2021